OXFORD STUDENT TEXTS

Series Editor: Victor Lee

Songs Of Innocence
And Of Experience

William Blake

Songs of Innocence and of Experience

Edited by Richard Willmott

Oxford University Press

OXFORD
UNIVERSITY PRESS
Great Clarendon Street, Oxford OX2 6DP

Oxford University Press is a department of the University of Oxford.
It furthers the University's objective of excellence in research, scholarship,
and education by publishing worldwide in

Oxford New York

Auckland Cape Town Dar es Salaam Hong Kong Karachi Kuala Lumpur
Madrid Melbourne Mexico City Nairobi New Delhi Taipei Toronto
Shanghai

With offices in
Argentina Austria Brazil Chile Czech Republic France Greece
Guatemala Hungary Italy Japan Poland Portugal Singapore
South Korea Switzerland Thailand Turkey Ukraine Vietnam

Oxford is a registered trade mark of Oxford University Press
in the UK and in certain other countries

ISBN-13: 978-0-19-831952-8
ISBN-10: 0-19-831952-5

Typeset by Koford Prints (Singapore) Pte. Ltd.
Printed in China

Other titles in the series

Contents

Acknowledgements

The text and order followed in this edition are those of Michael Mason's *William Blake*, in The Oxford Authors series. Although the order of Blake's poems varies in different copies, various groupings remain constant, and the Mason edition tries to be faithful to as many of these as possible.

My indebtedness, not only to Michael Mason, but also to a great many other editors and critics, will be apparent to all who are familiar with Blake studies. Apart from those mentioned in either the notes or bibliography, I should like to record how helpful W.H. Stevenson's notes were in the Stevenson and Erdman edition of *The Complete Poems* (Harlow) 1971.

Above all I should like to thank Dr Victor Lee, the general editor of this series, for his guidance and encouragement.

Richard Willmott

Dedication

Sydney Evans 1915 — 1988
Giles Evans 1949 — 1988

Man was made for joy and woe,
And when this we rightly know
Through the world we safely go.
(Auguries of Innocence)

The publishers would like to thank the Trianon Press for permission to reproduce Blake's engravings.

The text for the poems is take from *Blake A Selection* ed. Mason in the Oxford Authors series, by permission of the Academic Division of O.U.P.

The cover illustration is by John Rushton.

Editors

Dr Victor Lee

Victor Lee, the series editor, read English at University College, Cardiff. He was later awarded his doctorate at the University of Oxford. He has taught at secondary and tertiary level, and is currently working at the Open University. There, he has been involved in the making of a considerable number of texts, television and radio programmes. Victor Lee's experience as an examiner is very wide: he has been a Chief Examiner in English at 'A' level for three different boards stretching over a period of twenty years.

Richard Willmott

Richard Willmott read English at St. John's College, Cambridge, and then read a second degree in European Studies at the University of East Anglia whilst teaching at Norwich School. Subsequently he taught at the Manchester Grammar School before moving as head of English to Brighton College. He is currently head of the Dixie Grammar School. He has published articles on the influence of translations from Latin and French on seventeenth-century literature as well as two books on metaphysical poetry.

Foreword

Oxford Student Texts are specifically aimed at presenting poetry and drama to an audience which is studying English Literature at an advanced level. Each text is designed as an integrated whole consisting of three parts. The poetry or the play is always placed first to stress its importance and to encourage students to enjoy it without secondary critical material of any kind. When help is needed on other occasions, the second and third parts of these texts, the Notes and the Approaches, provide it.

The Notes perform two functions. Firstly, they provide information and explain allusions. Secondly, and this is where they differ from most texts at this level, they often raise questions of central concern to the interpretation of the poem or the play being dealt with, particularly in the use of a 'general note' placed at the beginning of the particular notes.

The third part, the Approaches section, deals with major issues of response to the particular selection of poetry or drama as opposed to the work of the writer as a whole. One of the major aims of this part of the text is to emphasize that there is no one right answer to interpretations, but a series of approaches. The reader is given guidance as to what counts as evidence, but, in the end, left to make up their mind as to which are the most suitable interpretations, or to add their own.

To help achieve this, the Approaches section contains a number of activity-discussion sequences, although it must be stressed that these are optional. Significant issues about the poetry or the play are raised in these activities. The reader is invited to tackle these activities before proceeding to the discussion section where possible responses to the questions raised in the activities are considered. Their main function is to engage the reader actively in the ideas of the text. However, these activity-discussion sequences are so arranged that, if the reader wishes to treat the Approaches as continuous prose and not attempt the activities, they can.

At the end of each text there is also a list of tasks. Whereas the activity-discussion sequences are aimed at increasing understanding of the literary work itself, these tasks are intended to help explore ideas about the poetry or the play after the student has completed the reading of the work and the studying of the Notes and Approaches. These tasks are particularly helpful for coursework projects or in preparing for an examination.

Victor Lee
Series Editor

Songs of Innocence (1789)

Introduction

Piping down the valleys wild,
Piping songs of pleasant glee,
On a cloud I saw a child,
And he laughing said to me:

'Pipe a song about a lamb.'
So I piped with merry cheer.
'Piper, pipe that song again.'
So I piped; he wept to hear.

'Drop thy pipe, thy happy pipe;
10 Sing thy songs of happy cheer.'
So I sung the same again,
While he wept with joy to hear.

'Piper sit thee down and write
In a book that all may read –'
So he vanished from my sight.
And I plucked a hollow reed,

And I made a rural pen,
And I stained the water clear,
And I wrote my happy songs
20 Every child may joy to hear.

A Dream

Once a dream did weave a shade
O'er my angel-guarded bed,
That an emmet lost its way
Where on grass methought I lay.

Troubled, wildered and forlorn,
Dark, benighted, travel-worn,
Over many a tangled spray
All heart-broke I heard her say:

'Oh my children! Do they cry?
10 Do they hear their father sigh?
Now they look abroad to see,
Now return and weep for me.'

Pitying I dropped a tear;
But I saw a glow-worm near,
Who replied: 'What wailing wight
Calls the watchman of the night?

'I am set to light the ground,
While the beetle goes his round.
Follow now the beetle's hum.
20 Little wanderer hie thee home.'

The Little Girl Lost

In futurity
I prophetic see
That the earth from sleep
(Grave the sentence deep)

Shall arise and seek
For her maker meek,
And the desert wild
Become a garden mild.

In the southern clime,
10   Where the summer's prime
Never fades away,
Lovely Lyca lay.

Seven summers old
Lovely Lyca told;
She had wandered long,
Hearing wild birds' song.

'Sweet sleep come to me
Underneath this tree;
Do father, mother weep?
20   Where can Lyca sleep?

'Lost in desert wild
Is your little child.
How can Lyca sleep,
If her mother weep?

'If her heart does ache,
Then let Lyca wake;
If my mother sleep,
Lyca shall not weep.

'Frowning, frowning night,
30 O'er this desert bright,
Let thy moon arise
While I close my eyes.'

Sleeping Lyca lay,
While the beasts of prey,
Come from caverns deep,
Viewed the maid asleep.

The kingly lion stood
And the virgin viewed,
Then he gambolled round
40 O'er the hallowed ground.

Leopards, tigers play,
Round her as she lay,
While the lion old
Bowed his mane of gold,

And her bosom lick,
And upon her neck;
From his eyes of flame
Ruby tears there came;

While the lioness
50 Loosed her slender dress
And naked they conveyed
To caves the sleeping maid.

The Little Girl Found

All the night in woe
Lyca's parents go,
Over valleys deep
While the deserts weep.

Tired and woe-begone,
Hoarse with making moan,
Arm in arm seven days
They traced the desert ways.

Seven nights they sleep
10 Among shadows deep,
And dream they see their child
Starved in desert wild.

Pale through pathless ways
The fancied image strays,
Famished, weeping, weak,
With hollow piteous shriek.

Rising from unrest,
The trembling woman pressed
With feet of weary woe;
20 She could no further go.

In his arms he bore
Her, armed with sorrow sore,
Till before their way
A couching lion lay.

Turning back was vain.
Soon his heavy mane
Bore them to the ground;
Then he stalked around,

Smelling to his prey;
30 But their fears allay
When he licks their hands,
And silent by them stands.

They look upon his eyes,
Filled with deep surprise,
And wondering behold
A spirit armed in gold.

On his head a crown,
On his shoulders down
Flowed his golden hair.
40 Gone was all their care.

'Follow me,' he said,
'Weep not for the maid;
In my palace deep,
Lyca lies asleep.'

Then they followèd
Where the vision led,
And saw their sleeping child,
Among tigers wild.

To this day they dwell
50 In a lonely dell,
Nor fear the wolvish howl,
Nor the lion's growl.

The Blossom

Merry, merry sparrow,
Under leaves so green,
A happy blossom
Sees you swift as arrow
Seek your cradle narrow
Near my bosom.

Pretty, pretty robin,
Under leaves so green,
A happy blossom
10 Hears you sobbing, sobbing,
Pretty, pretty robin
Near my bosom.

The Lamb

Little Lamb who made thee?
Dost thou know who made thee?
Gave thee life and bid thee feed
By the stream and o'er the mead;
Gave thee clothing of delight,
Softest clothing woolly bright;
Gave thee such a tender voice,
Making all the vales rejoice.
Little Lamb who made thee?
10   Dost thou know who made thee?

Little Lamb I'll tell thee,
Little Lamb I'll tell thee:
He is callèd by thy name,
For he calls himself a lamb.
He is meek and he is mild;
He became a little child.
I a child and thou a lamb,
We are callèd by his name.
Little Lamb God bless thee.
20   Little Lamb God bless thee.

The Shepherd

How sweet is the shepherd's sweet lot!
From the morn to the evening he strays;
He shall follow his sheep all the day,
And his tongue shall be fillèd with praise.

For he hears the lamb's innocent call,
And he hears the ewe's tender reply.
He is watchful, while they are in peace,
For they know when their shepherd is nigh.

Infant Joy

'I have no name;
I am but two days old.'
What shall I call thee?
'I happy am;
Joy is my name.'
Sweet joy befall thee!

Pretty joy!
Sweet joy but two days old,
Sweet joy I call thee.
10 Thou dost smile;
I sing the while.
Sweet joy befall thee.

On Another's Sorrow

Can I see another's woe,
And not be in sorrow too?
Can I see another's grief
And not seek for kind relief?

Can I see a falling tear,
And not feel my sorrow's share?
Can a father see his child
Weep, nor be with sorrow filled?

Can a mother sit, and hear
10   An infant groan, an infant fear?
No, no, never can it be.
Never, never can it be.

And can he who smiles on all
Hear the wren with sorrows small,
Hear the small bird's grief and care,
Hear the woes that infants bear –

And not sit beside the nest,
Pouring pity in their breast;
And not sit the cradle near
20   Weeping tear on infant's tear;

And not sit both night and day,
Wiping all our tears away?
Oh no! never can it be.
Never, never can it be.

He doth give his joy to all.
He becomes an infant small.
He becomes a man of woe.
He doth feel the sorrow too.

Think not thou canst sigh a sigh,
30   And thy maker is not by.
Think not thou canst weep a tear,
And thy maker is not near.

Oh! he gives to us his joy,
That our grief he may destroy,
Till our grief is fled and gone
He doth sit by us and moan.

Spring

Sound the flute!
Now it's mute.
Birds delight
Day and night.
Nightingale
In the dale,
Lark in sky,
Merrily,
Merrily, merrily to welcome in the year.

10   Little boy
Full of joy,
Little girl
Sweet and small.
Cock does crow,
So do you.
Merry voice,
Infant noise,
Merrily, merrily to welcome in the year.

Little lamb
20   Here I am.
Come and lick
My white neck.
Let me pull
Your soft wool.
Let me kiss
Your soft face,
Merrily, merrily we welcome in the year.

The Schoolboy

I love to rise in a summer morn,
When the birds sing on every tree;
The distant huntsman winds his horn,
And the skylark sings with me.
Oh! what sweet company.

But to go to school in a summer morn,
Oh! it drives all joy away;
Under a cruel eye outworn,
The little ones spend the day
10   In sighing and dismay.

Ah! then at times I drooping sit,
And spend many an anxious hour,
Nor in my book can I take delight,
Nor sit in learning's bower,
Worn through with the dreary shower.

How can the bird that is born for joy
Sit in a cage and sing?
How can a child when fears annoy
But droop his tender wing,
20   And forget his youthful spring?

O father and mother! if buds are nipped,
And blossoms blown away,
And if the tender plants are stripped
Of their joy in the springing day,
By sorrow and care's dismay,

How shall the summer arise in joy,
Or the summer fruits appear?
Or how shall we gather what griefs destroy,
Or bless the mellowing year,
30 When the blasts of winter appear?

Laughing Song

When the green woods laugh with the voice of joy
And the dimpling stream runs laughing by,
When the air does laugh with our merry wit
And the green hill laughs with the noise of it,

When the meadows laugh with lively green
And the grasshopper laughs in the merry scene,
When Mary and Susan and Emily
With their sweet round mouths sing 'Ha, Ha, He,'

When the painted birds laugh in the shade
10 Where our table with cherries and nuts is spread –
Come live and be merry and join with me,
To sing the sweet chorus of 'Ha, Ha, He.'

The Little Black Boy

My mother bore me in the southern wild,
And I am black, but oh! my soul is white.
White as an angel is the English child;
But I am black as if bereaved of light.

My mother taught me underneath a tree,
And sitting down before the heat of day
She took me on her lap and kissèd me,
And pointing to the east began to say:

'Look on the rising sun! There God does live,
10   And gives his light and gives his heat away;
And flowers and trees and beasts and men receive
Comfort in morning, joy in the noon day.

'And we are put on earth a little space,
That we may learn to bear the beams of love;
And these black bodies and this sun-burnt face
Is but a cloud, and like a shady grove.

'For when our souls have learned the heat to bear
The cloud will vanish; we shall hear his voice,
Saying: "Come out from the grove my love and care,
20   And round my golden tent like lambs rejoice." '

Thus did my mother say and kissèd me,
And thus I say to little English boy.
When I from black and he from white cloud free,
And round the tent of God like lambs we joy,

I'll shade him from the heat till he can bear
To lean in joy upon our father's knee,
And then I'll stand and stroke his silver hair
And be like him, and he will then love me.

The Voice of the Ancient Bard

Youth of delight come hither
And see the opening morn,
Image of truth new-born.
Doubt is fled and clouds of reason,
Dark disputes and artful teasing.
Folly is an endless maze;
Tangled roots perplex her ways.
How many have fallen there!
They stumble all night over bones of the dead,
10 And feel they know not what but care,
And wish to lead others when they should be led.

The Echoing Green

The sun does arise,
And make happy the skies.
The merry bells ring
To welcome the spring.
The skylark and thrush,
The birds of the bush,
Sing louder around,
To the bells' cheerful sound,
While our sports shall be seen
10 On the echoing green.

Old John with white hair
Does laugh away care,
Sitting under the oak,
Among the old folk.
They laugh at our play,
And soon they all say:
'Such, such were the joys
When we all, girls and boys,
In our youth-time were seen
20 On the echoing green.'

Till the little ones weary
No more can be merry;
The sun does descend,
And our sports have an end.
Round the laps of their mothers
Many sisters and brothers,
Like birds in their nest,
Are ready for rest;
And sport no more seen
30 On the darkening green.

Nurse's Song

When the voices of children are heard on the green
And laughing is heard on the hill,
My heart is at rest within my breast
And everything else is still.

'Then come home my children: the sun is gone down
And the dews of night arise.
Come, come leave off play and let us away,
Till the morning appears in the skies.'

'No, no let us play, for it is yet day
10   And we cannot go to sleep.
Besides, in the sky the little birds fly,
And the hills are all covered with sheep.'

'Well, well go and play till the light fades away,
And then go home to bed.'
The little ones leaped and shouted and laughed
And all the hills echoèd.

Holy Thursday

'Twas on a Holy Thursday, their innocent faces
    clean,
The children walking two and two in red and blue
    and green,
Grey headed beadles walked before with wands as
    white as snow;
Till into the high dome of Paul's they like Thames
    waters flow.

Oh what a multitude they seemed, these flowers of
    London town.
Seated in companies they sit, with radiance all their
    own.
The hum of multitudes was there, but multitudes of
    lambs:
Thousands of little boys and girls raising their
    innocent hands.

Now like a mighty wind they raise to Heaven the
    voice of song,
10 Or like harmonious thunderings the seats of
    Heaven among.
Beneath them sit the agèd men, wise guardians of
    the poor.
Then cherish pity, lest you drive an angel from your
    door.

The Divine Image

To Mercy, Pity, Peace and Love
All pray in their distress,
And to these virtues of delight
Return their thankfulness.

For Mercy, Pity, Peace and Love
Is God our father dear,
And Mercy, Pity, Peace and Love
Is Man his child and care.

For Mercy has a human heart,
10   Pity a human face,
And Love the human form divine,
And Peace the human dress.

Then every man of every clime
That prays in his distress,
Prays to the human form divine:
Love, Mercy, Pity, Peace.

And all must love the human form,
In heathen, Turk or Jew.
Where Mercy, Love and Pity dwell,
20   There God is dwelling too.

The Chimney-Sweeper

When my mother died I was very young,
And my father sold me while yet my tongue
Could scarcely cry, 'weep weep weep weep'.
So your chimneys I sweep and in soot I sleep.

There's little Tom Dacre, who cried when his head,
That curled like a lamb's back, was shaved, so I said:
'Hush Tom, never mind it, for when your head's
    bare,
You know that the soot cannot spoil your white hair.'

And so he was quiet, and that very night,
10 As Tom was a-sleeping, he had such a sight:
That thousands of sweepers, Dick, Joe, Ned and Jack,
Were all of them locked up in coffins of black,

And by came an angel who had a bright key,
And he opened the coffins and set them all free.
Then down a green plain leaping, laughing they run,
And wash in a river and shine in the sun.

Then naked and white, all their bags left behind,
They rise upon clouds, and sport in the wind.
And the angel told Tom if he'd be a good boy,
20 He'd have God for his father and never want joy.

And so Tom awoke, and we rose in the dark,
And got with our bags and our brushes to work.
Though the morning was cold, Tom was happy and
    warm.
So if all do their duty, they need not fear harm.

A Cradle Song

Sweet dreams, form a shade
O'er my lovely infant's head,
Sweet dreams of pleasant streams,
By happy, silent, moony beams.

Sweet sleep, with soft down
Weave thy brows an infant crown.
Sweet sleep, angel mild,
Hover o'er my happy child.

Sweet smiles in the night,
10 Hover over my delight.
Sweet smiles, mother's smiles,
All the livelong night beguiles.

Sweet moans, dovelike sighs,
Chase not slumber from thy eyes.
Sweet moans, sweeter smiles,
All the dovelike moans beguiles.

Sleep, sleep happy child.
All creation slept and smiled.
Sleep, sleep, happy sleep,
20 While o'er thee thy mother weep.

Sweet babe, in thy face,
Holy image I can trace.
Sweet babe, once like thee
Thy maker lay, and wept for me,

Wept for me, for thee, for all,
When he was an infant small.
Thou his image ever see,
Heavenly face that smiles on thee,

Smiles on thee, on me, on all,
30 Who became an infant small.
Infant smiles are his own smiles;
Heaven and earth to peace beguiles.

The Little Boy Lost

'Father, father where are you going?
Oh do not walk so fast.
Speak father, speak to your little boy,
Or else I shall be lost.'

The night was dark, no father was there,
The child was wet with dew.
The mire was deep, and the child did weep,
And away the vapour flew.

The Little Boy Found

The little boy lost in the lonely fen,
Led by the wand'ring light,
Began to cry, but God ever nigh
Appeared like his father in white.

He kissed the child and by the hand led,
And to his mother brought,
Who in sorrow pale through the lonely dale
Her little boy weeping sought.

Night

The sun descending in the west,
The evening star does shine.
The birds are silent in their nest,
And I must seek for mine.
The moon, like a flower
In heaven's high bower,
With silent delight
Sits and smiles on the night.

Farewell green fields and happy groves,
10 Where flocks have took delight;
Where lambs have nibbled, silent moves
The feet of angels bright.
Unseen they pour blessing,
And joy without ceasing,
On each bud and blossom,
And each sleeping bosom.

They look in every thoughtless nest,
Where birds are covered warm;
They visit caves of every beast,
20 To keep them all from harm.
If they see any weeping
That should have been sleeping,
They pour sleep on their head
And sit down by their bed.

When wolves and tigers howl for prey
They pitying stand and weep,
Seeking to drive their thirst away,
And keep them from the sheep.
But if they rush dreadful,
30 The angels most heedful,
Receive each mild spirit,
New worlds to inherit.

And there the lion's ruddy eyes
Shall flow with tears of gold,
And pitying the tender cries
And walking round the fold,
Saying: 'Wrath by his meekness,
And by his health sickness,
Is driven away
40 From our immortal day.

'And now beside thee, bleating lamb,
I can lie down and sleep,
Or think on him who bore thy name,
Graze after thee and weep.
For washed in life's river,
My bright mane for ever
Shall shine like the gold,
As I guard o'er the fold.'

Songs of Experience (1793)

Introduction

Hear the voice of the bard!
Who present, past, and future sees;
Whose ears have heard
The Holy Word,
That walked among the ancient trees

Calling the lapsèd soul,
And weeping in the evening dew;
That might control
The starry pole,
10 And fallen, fallen light renew!

'O Earth, O Earth return!
Arise from out the dewy grass.
Night is worn,
And the morn
Rises from the slumberous mass.

'Turn away no more;
Why wilt thou turn away?
The starry floor,
The wat'ry shore,
20 Is giv'n thee till the break of day.'

Earth's Answer

Earth raised up her head
From the darkness dread and drear.
Her light fled –
Stony dread! –
And her locks covered with grey despair.

'Prisoned on wat'ry shore
Starry jealousy does keep my den.
Cold and hoar,
Weeping o'er,
10   I hear the father of the ancient men.

'Selfish father of men,
Cruel, jealous, selfish fear!
Can delight
Chained in night
The virgins of youth and morning bear?

'Does spring hide its joy
When buds and blossoms grow?
Does the sower
Sow by night?
20   Or the ploughman in darkness plough?

'Break this heavy chain
That does freeze my bones around.
Selfish! Vain!
Eternal bane!
That free love with bondage bound.'

The Clod and the Pebble

'Love seeketh not itself to please,
Nor for itself hath any care,
But for another gives its ease,
And builds a Heaven in Hell's despair.'

So sang a little Clod of Clay,
Trodden with the cattle's feet,
But a Pebble of the brook
Warbled out these metres meet:

'Love seeketh only self to please,
10   To bind another to its delight,
Joys in another's loss of ease,
And builds a Hell in Heaven's despite.'

Holy Thursday

Is this a holy thing to see,
In a rich and fruitful land:
Babes reduced to misery,
Fed with cold and usurous hand?

Is that trembling cry a song?
Can it be a song of joy?
And so many children poor?
It is a land of poverty!

29

And their sun does never shine,
10 And their fields are bleak and bare,
And their ways are filled with thorns;
It is eternal winter there.

For where'er the sun does shine,
And where'er the rain does fall –
Babe can never hunger there,
Nor poverty the mind appal.

The Chimney-Sweeper

A little black thing among the snow,
Crying 'weep, weep' in notes of woe!
'Where are thy father and mother? Say!'
'They are both gone up to the church to pray.

'Because I was happy upon the heath,
And smiled among the winter's snow,
They clothed me in the clothes of death,
And taught me to sing the notes of woe.

'And because I am happy and dance and sing,
10 They think they have done me no injury,
And are gone to praise God and his priest and king,
Who make up a heaven of our misery.'

Nurse's Song

When the voices of children are heard on the green,
And whisperings are in the dale,
The days of my youth rise fresh in my mind,
My face turns green and pale.

Then come home my children, the sun is gone down,
And the dews of night arise.
Your spring and your day are wasted in play,
And your winter and night in disguise.

The Sick Rose

O rose, thou art sick;
The invisible worm
That flies in the night,
In the howling storm,

Has found out thy bed
Of crimson joy,
And his dark secret love
Does thy life destroy.

The Fly

Little fly,
Thy summer's play
My thoughtless hand
Has brushed away.

Am not I
A fly like thee?
Or art not thou
A man like me?

For I dance
10 And drink and sing,
Till some blind hand
Shall brush my wing.

If thought is life
And strength and breath,
And the want
Of thought is death,

Then am I
A happy fly,
If I live,
20 Or if I die.

The Angel

I dreamt a dream! – What can it mean! –
And that I was a maiden queen,
Guarded by an angel mild.
Witless woe was ne'er beguiled!

And I wept both night and day,
And he wiped my tears away,
And I wept both day and night,
And hid from him my heart's delight.

So he took his wings and fled;
10   Then the morn blushed rosy red.
I dried my tears, and armed my fear
With ten thousand shields and spears.

Soon my angel came again.
I was armed; he came in vain,
For the time of youth was fled,
And grey hairs were on my head.

The Tiger

Tiger, tiger, burning bright,
In the forests of the night:
What immortal hand or eye
Could frame thy fearful symmetry?

In what distant deeps or skies,
Burnt the fire of thine eyes?
On what wings dare he aspire?
What the hand dare seize the fire?

And what shoulder, and what art,
10 Could twist the sinews of thy heart?
And when thy heart began to beat,
What dread hand? and what dread feet?

What the hammer? what the chain?
In what furnace was thy brain?
What the anvil? what dread grasp
Dare its deadly terrors clasp?

When the stars threw down their spears,
And watered Heaven with their tears,
Did he smile his work to see?
20 Did he who made the lamb make thee?

Tiger, tiger, burning bright,
In the forests of the night:
What immortal hand or eye
Dare frame thy fearful symmetry?

My Pretty Rose Tree

A flower was offered to me,
Such a flower as May never bore,
But I said, 'I've a pretty rose tree,'
And I passed the sweet flower o'er.

Then I went to my pretty rose tree,
To tend her by day and by night,
But my rose turned away with jealousy,
And her thorns were my only delight.

Ah! Sunflower

Ah! sunflower, weary of time,
Who countest the steps of the sun,
Seeking after that sweet golden clime
Where the traveller's journey is done;

Where the youth pined away with desire,
And the pale virgin shrouded in snow,
Arise from their graves and aspire;
Where my sunflower wishes to go.

The Lily

The modest rose puts forth a thorn,
The humble sheep a threat'ning horn;
While the lily white shall in love delight,
Nor a thorn nor a threat stain her beauty bright.

The Garden of Love

I went to the Garden of Love,
And saw what I never had seen:
A chapel was built in the midst,
Where I used to play on the green.

And the gates of this chapel were shut,
And 'Thou shalt not' writ over the door;
So I turned to the Garden of Love,
That so many sweet flowers bore.

And I saw it was filled with graves,
10   And tomb-stones where flowers should be,
And priests in black gowns were walking their rounds,
And binding with briars my joys and desires.

The Little Vagabond

Dear mother, dear mother, the church is cold,
But the ale-house is healthy and pleasant and warm.
Besides, I can tell where I am used well;
Such usage in Heaven will never do well.

But if at the church they would give us some ale,
And a pleasant fire our souls to regale,
We'd sing and we'd pray all the live-long day,
Nor ever once wish from the church to stray.

Then the parson might preach and drink and sing,
10 And we'd be as happy as birds in the spring;
And modest dame Lurch, who is always at church,
Would not have bandy children, nor fasting, nor
    birch.

And God, like a father rejoicing to see
His children as pleasant and happy as he,
Would have no more quarrel with the Devil or the
    barrel,
But kiss him and give him both drink and apparel.

London

I wander through each chartered street,
Near where the chartered Thames does flow,
And mark in every face I meet
Marks of weakness, marks of woe.

In every cry of every man,
In every infant's cry of fear,
In every voice, in every ban,
The mind-forged manacles I hear:

How the chimney-sweeper's cry
10 Every black'ning church appalls,
And the hapless soldier's sigh
Runs in blood down palace walls.

But most through midnight streets I hear
How the youthful harlot's curse
Blasts the new-born infant's tear,
And blights with plagues the marriage hearse.

The Human Abstract

Pity would be no more
If we did not make somebody poor,
And Mercy no more could be
If all were as happy as we.

And mutual fear brings Peace,
Till the selfish loves increase.
Then Cruelty knits a snare,
And spreads his baits with care.

He sits down with holy fears,
10 And waters the ground with tears;
Then Humility takes its root
Underneath his foot.

Soon spreads the dismal shade
Of Mystery over his head,
And the caterpillar and fly
Feed on the Mystery.

And it bears the fruit of Deceit,
Ruddy and sweet to eat,
And the raven his nest has made
20 In its thickest shade.

The gods of the earth and sea
Sought through Nature to find this tree,
But their search was all in vain.
There grows one in the human brain.

Infant Sorrow

My mother groaned, my father wept!
Into the dangerous world I leapt,
Helpless, naked, piping loud,
Like a fiend hid in a cloud.

Struggling in my father's hands,
Striving against my swaddling bands,
Bound and weary, I thought best
To sulk upon my mother's breast.

A Poison Tree

I was angry with my friend;
I told my wrath – my wrath did end.
I was angry with my foe;
I told it not – my wrath did grow.

And I watered it in fears,
Night and morning with my tears,
And I sunnèd it with smiles,
And with soft deceitful wiles.

And it grew both day and night,
10   Till it bore an apple bright.
And my foe beheld it shine,
And he knew that it was mine,

And into my garden stole
When the night had veiled the pole.
In the morning glad I see
My foe outstretched beneath the tree.

A Little Boy Lost

'Nought loves another as itself,
Nor venerates another so,
Nor is it possible to thought
A greater than itself to know.

'And father, how can I love you,
Or any of my brothers more?
I love you like the little bird
That picks up crumbs around the door.'

The priest sat by and heard the child;
10   In trembling zeal he seized his hair.
He led him by his little coat,
And all admired the priestly care.

And, standing on the altar high,
'Lo, what a fiend is here!' said he,
'One who sets reason up for judge
Of our most holy mystery.'

The weeping child could not be heard;
The weeping parents wept in vain.
They stripped him to his little shirt,
20   And bound him in an iron chain,

And burned him in a holy place,
Where many had been burned before.
The weeping parents wept in vain.
Are such things done on Albion's shore?

A Little Girl Lost

Children of the future age,
Reading this indignant page,
Know that in a former time
Love! sweet love! was thought a crime.

In the age of gold,
Free from winter's cold,
Youth and maiden bright,
To the holy light,
Naked in the sunny beams delight.

10   Once a youthful pair,
Filled with softest care,
Met in garden bright,
Where the holy light
Had just removed the curtains of the night.

There in rising day
On the grass they play.
Parents were afar;
Strangers came not near;
And the maiden soon forgot her fear.

20   Tired with kisses sweet,
They agree to meet
When the silent sleep
Waves o'er heavens deep,
And the weary, tired wanderers weep.

To her father white
Came the maiden bright;
But his loving look,
Like the holy book,
All her tender limbs with terror shook.

30   'Ona! pale and weak!
     To thy father speak.
     Oh the trembling fear!
     Oh the dismal care,
     That shakes the blossoms of my hoary hair!'

To Tirzah

     Whate'er is born of mortal birth
     Must be consumèd with the earth,
     To rise from generation free.
     Then what have I to do with thee?

     The sexes sprung from shame and pride,
     Blowed in the morn, in evening died.
     But mercy changed death into sleep;
     The sexes rose to work and weep.

     Thou, mother of my mortal part,
10   With cruelty didst mould my heart,
     And with false self-deceiving tears
     Didst bind my nostrils, eyes and ears;

     Didst close my tongue in senseless clay,
     And me to mortal life betray.
     The death of Jesus set me free.
     Then what have I to do with thee?

A Divine Image

Cruelty has a human heart,
And Jealousy a human face;
Terror the human form divine,
And Secrecy the human dress.

The human dress is forgèd iron;
The human form, a fiery forge;
The human face, a furnace sealed;
The human heart, its hungry gorge.

Notes

Songs of Innocence

Introduction

This poem presents in simple narrative form the initial inspiration to write *Songs of Innocence*. There is a progression from a tune without words, to a song, to the final writing down of the poem. Is this merely an account of the creative process, or is there a sense of loss once the initial inspiration has been fixed and set down on paper? – after all the child disappears. See note on line 18.

The poem is written in seven syllable lines starting with a strong stress (e.g. PIping DOWN the VALLeys WILD). It is the same rhythm as in *The Tiger*. Is the effect on the mood similar or not? Should the *And*'s at the end of the poem be stressed, or should there be a light skipping rhythm with the first stresses in each line coming on *plucked, stained, made* and *wrote*? (Contrast with the repeated *And*'s of *A Poison Tree*.)

The frontispiece to *Innocence* illustrates the poem literally, showing the poet as a shepherd with his sheep behind him and a pipe in his hand, looking up to the child on a cloud. There is a long tradition going back to Greek and Latin literature associating pastoral poetry (the simple poetry of the shepherd – *pastor* is the Latin for shepherd) with an idealized Golden Age of peace and innocence.

5 **lamb** Blake used a capital L here, which may suggest a reference to Jesus, although the use of the indefinite article suggests rather any innocent subject. For the linking of child and lamb (both symbols of innocence) with the infant Jesus see *The Lamb* (p.7).

8 **wept** But note that in 9 he calls the pipe *happy* and that in 12 he wept *with joy*.

17 **rural pen** The simple country pen is made from the *hollow reed*.

18 The water is *stained* to make the ink or the watercolour for the poems. It could be argued that the *staining* of the *water clear* represents the loss of the original purity of vision once it is put into words, but against this must be set Blake's claim that his poems are *happy songs Every child may joy to hear*.

A Dream

Does the fact that this picture of security is a dream enhance the sense of innocence, or suggest a lack of reality?

1 **shade** A protective covering.
3 **emmet** Ant.
5 **wildered** Lost (and possibly also *bewildered*).
15 **wight** Creature.
20 **hie thee** Go quickly.

The Little Girl Lost and The Little Girl Found

These two poems were originally in *Innocence*, although omitted from some copies, but were later placed by Blake in *Experience* in all but one of the combined copies. The sources of the poems have given rise to much speculation. There are elements which seem to be derived from fairy tales such as *Sleeping Beauty*, *Snow White* and *Beauty and the Beast*. There are also echoes of the story of Persephone who was carried off to the kingdom of the dead by Hades and searched for by her mother Demeter, the goddess of the harvest; this story is related to the seasons: when Persephone is in the Underworld there is winter as her mother Demeter (or Ceres) will let nothing grow, and when she is released to the upper world summer and harvest come. There is, however, an alternative neo-Platonist interpretation (see Approaches p.108) which sees the poem as a myth of the pre-existent soul entering into life.

A further interpretation suggests that it is about Innocence entering upon sexual Experience (after all *A Little Girl Lost* – the contrary song in *Experience* – is about the opposite, namely a father's forbidding his daughter to enjoy natural, uninhibited love). Certainly the illustration on the first page shows a girl who looks much older than seven embracing a youth. On the other hand this illustration could be taken not as a portrayal of Lyca, but as a representation of the world restored to the paradisal condition of the Garden of Eden (see the first two stanzas) in which sexual experience is not incompatible with innocence – after all the serpent appears to have turned away baffled. The illustration of the final page shows a mature and naked Lyca lying asleep in the presence of a lion and lioness, with whom young naked children are playing, while to one side two trees are twined together (in a symbol of love?).

The Little Girl Lost

1-8   In a number of the combined copies Blake placed this poem in *Experience* just after *Introduction* and *Earth's Answer*. How does the mood expressed in these first two stanzas compare with that of the other two poems?

4   **Grave** If this is a verb it means *engrave* (i.e. the poet's prophetic words are so important that they should be deeply engraved); if it is an adjective then the *sentence* of *sleep* that has been passed on the earth is both serious (*grave*) and profound (*deep*).

7-8   In *Isaiah* 35, 1 there is a picture of an ideal time in which the *desert shall rejoice, and blossom as the rose*. Also the return of Persephone to the earth brings about the spring.

17-32   These lines are the words of Lyca, although 20 is a question that Lyca imagines her worried parents asking.

18   **this tree** The second illustration shows Lyca lying beneath what is perhaps an elm tree, the tree sacred to the god of sleep that was said to grow at the entrance to the Underworld.

21   **desert wild** As in 7; should the stress be on *desert* (which is barren before Lyca moves to sexual experience), or on *wild* (a place of danger), or on both as typifying the present condition of the world before its restoration to a *garden mild*? Alternatively does the earlier *wild/mild* rhyme (7-8) remove the threat from *wild* in 21?

23-4   These lines seem heartless if taken literally, but could suggest parental inhibitions against sexual love (compare *A Little Girl Lost* in which the father's *loving look … All her tender limbs with terror shook* – p. 42). Alternatively they could suggest the misery of the world in its present condition that prevents a return to a more blissful state. The neo-Platonist interpretation is that Demeter, the mother, represents intellect and is weeping because she does not wish her daughter Persephone, representing the soul, to enter the world of material existence.

30 **bright** Despite Blake's comma after this word, it seems reasonable to assume that it describes *moon* rather than *desert*.

50 **slender dress** Taking off the dress could imply leaving the body in death, or sexual experience, or a return to a natural and paradisal innocence.

The Little Girl Found

14 **the fancied image** The mistaken image that the parents have of Lyca; in pursuing this image the plight of the adults might be compared to that of the little boy *led by the wand'ring light* (see *The Little Boy Found* p.23).

18 **pressed** Either hurried (pressed on), or possibly halted (her feet pressed to the ground without moving).

22 **armed** The father carries no weapon, but only sorrow and the sorrowing mother (or perhaps *armed* describes the mother).

30 **allay** calm down.

33-40 How might this transformation of the savage lion into a spirit of power and dignity tie in with the interpretations of the poems suggested in the headnote?

51-2 Is there an echo here of the lament for 'Fidele' in *Cymbeline* (Act 4, Scene 2) who, like Lyca, is mistakenly thought to be dead?

> Fear no more the heat o' the sun,
>   Nor the furious winter's rages;
> Thou thy worldly task has done,
>   Home art gone and ta'en thy wages.

The Blossom

Is the purpose of this poem to show the human speaker of the poem, the birds and the blossom all united in sharing simple emotions? Some critics have taken the illustration of a flame rising up the right hand side of the page to be phallic and have argued that the poem is a celebration of innocent physical love. Others point out that the illustration may well not have been conceived at the same time as the poem and that such an interpretation is inappropriate for a poem originally intended for children. A comparison with *The Sick Rose*, which is concerned with the corrupting effect of hidden passion, may help you to reach your own conclusion.

1-2   How do the first two lines of each verse relate to the sentence and
&   structure of the rest of the verse? Are the verses addressed to the
7-8   sparrow and robin respectively, or are the birds simply mentioned as part of a fluid description which ignores conventional grammatical structure?

The Lamb

Does this poem seem more childish than the others? What is the effect of posing questions in the first verse and answering them in the second? (See Approaches p. 119) The repetitions suggest that Blake may have intended this poem to be set to music, in which case its simplicity would not seem so obtrusive (simple lyrics are generally the most successful). Interestingly the composer Vaughan Williams referred to it as '*that beastly little lamb*', but nevertheless wrote a lovely setting for it, accompanied by a haunting oboe line. There is also an effectively simple, lullaby-like choral setting by John Tavener. If the poem still strikes you as irritatingly naïve, consider the way in which it embodies the ideas of creation and redemption (see note on 13) and relate it to *The Tiger*.

13   In this poem Blake appears to write as an orthodox Christian. God, who as creator made the lamb, is also Jesus, who as Lamb of God was sacrificed to save mankind from sin; hence the creator *calls himself a lamb*. Nevertheless in *The Tiger* Blake is to ask the question, *Did he who made the lamb make thee?*

16   God became man when he was born at Christmas.

18   Christians are named after Jesus Christ.

The Shepherd

The frontispiece picture of the piper/poet of *Introduction* standing in front of his sheep suggests that the poet himself is the shepherd delighting in the innocent sheep that he looks after. At the same time the imagery of Psalm 23 (*The Lord is my shepherd*) and of the parables of Jesus as the *good shepherd* who will *lay down his life for the sheep*, and whose *sheep follow him for they know his voice* (*John 10, 1–18*) inevitably comes to mind. As well as comparing the trusting relationship between shepherd and sheep to that between Jesus and his followers, compare it with that between the adults and children in *The Echoing Green* and *Nurse's Song* (*Innocence*). How do these relationships contrast with those in *A Little Boy Lost* and *Nurse's Song* (*Experience*)?

1 **lot** Destiny or allotted task in life.
4 Compare *Psalm 71, 7: O let my mouth be filled with thy praise: that I may sing of thy glory and honour all the day long.*

Infant Joy

This simple-seeming poem is perhaps best taken literally as a picture of uncomplicated and innocent love between mother and baby, but there are other ways of looking at it. One critic sees an attempt at realism in the imitation of the repetitive speech of the small child, but then takes up Coleridge's objection to the poem, namely that a two-day-old baby cannot speak. He then suggests that we see an attempt by an adult to manipulate innocence by imputing speech to the inarticulate child and imposing a name and character on it[1].

A second critic draws heavily on the illustration of the text (see p.140) to argue that the poem is about the consequences of consummating love. He sees the unopened bud at the left of the page as an unimpregnated womb and the open bud at the top of the page, which has a picture of a mother with her baby on her lap, as an

---

1. Edward Larrissy, *William Blake*, (Oxford) 1985.

impregnated womb. Mother and baby are being greeted by an angel just as the Virgin Mary was greeted by Gabriel at the Annunciation of the birth of Jesus; hence the argument that the baby shown here within the bud is newly conceived rather than born. The words of the second stanza may be spoken by either the messenger or the mother[2].

The annunication-like illustration coupled with the repetition of *I am* has led a third critic to offer another view of the poem. When Moses asks God his name the reply is: *I AM THAT I AM . . . Thus shalt thou say unto the children of Israel, I AM hath sent me unto you* (*Exodus 3,14*). Therefore when Jesus says to the Jews *Before Abraham was, I am* (*John 8, 58*) they interpret this correctly as a claim to divinity and take up stones to put him to death. This critic argues that by implication the infant is divine and that divinity is *joy*[3].

On Another's Sorrow

As in *A Dream* Blake here acknowledges the fact of grief, but offers consolation. In 22 he echoes a phrase which occurs twice in *The Revelation of St John the Divine*, on both occasions referring to *a new heaven and a new earth* (21,1), in which the sufferings of life in this world shall be brought to an end: *They shall hunger no more, neither thirst any more; neither shall the sun light on them, nor any heat. For the Lamb which is in the midst of the throne shall feed them, and shall lead them unto living fountains of waters: and God shall wipe away all tears from their eyes (7,16-17)*. Nevertheless the comfort offered is presented in immediate and human terms (see the last three stanzas and compare with *The Divine Image* on p. 19).

11-12 Are the repetitions here evidence of the speaker's confidence or of an underlying uncertainty that has to be repressed by emphatic

---

2. Geoffrey Keynes (ed.), *Blake, Songs of Innocence and of Experience*, (Oxford) 1970.
3. Alicia Ostriker (ed.), *William Blake: The Complete Poems*, (Harmondsworth) 1977.

assertion? Are both readings acceptable, depending on whether the poem is read by itself, or in the context of the *Songs* as a whole?

13   **he who smiles on all** Jesus (see 26-7).

14   **the wren** Compare Jesus's words: *Are not two sparrows sold for a farthing? and one of them shall not fall on the ground without your Father* (Matthew 10, 29) and *Behold the fowls of the air: for they sow not, neither do they reap, nor gather into barns; yet your heavenly Father feedeth them (Matthew 6, 26).*

26   Jesus is born as a human baby.

27-8   This echoes a passage in *Isaiah* which is taken by Christians to foreshadow the crucifixion of Jesus: *He is despised and rejected of men: a man of sorrows and acquainted with grief ... Surely he hath borne our griefs and carried our sorrows (53, 3-4).*

30   **maker** i.e. God in the human form of Jesus.

Spring

What is the effect of the rhythm? What other evidence is there to suggest that Blake may have intended this poem to be sung?

The mood of the poem is reflected in the exuberant twists and curls of foliage in the decoration. The bottom of the second page shows a small, naked child embracing a lamb; this is presumably the speaker of the third stanza.

The Schoolboy

This poem was transferred to *Experience* in a few of the combined copies. What elements in the poem might explain this change?

8   **outworn** Is the schoolmaster's eye aged or out of date?

14   **learning's bower** *Bower* can mean somewhere quiet and intimate (as in a lady's boudoir) and also a shelter made of plants in a garden. Neither the seclusion nor the contact with nature is available in the classroom, but both are perhaps found by the boy in the illustration who is comfortably ensconced at the top of a tree reading a book.

17   **cage** The classroom, his upbringing, or even the physical body (see Approaches pp. 108-9).

21   **buds** The start of an extended metaphor comparing children to plants. The appeal to the parents suggests that it is not only the schoolmaster who is a source of frosts to *nip* and gales to *blow*. What is the consequence in adulthood of such a misguided upbringing?

29   **mellowing** Ripening; there will be no harvest of *summer fruits* before the winter of old age sets in.

Laughing Song

Note the effect on the rhythm of the pairs of light, unstressed syllables. How successful is Blake in capturing the simplicity of innocent joy?

There are perhaps echoes of *Psalm* 65, which gives thanks for the richness of creation. *the little hills shall rejoice on every side . . . the valleys also shall stand so thick with corn, that they shall laugh and sing (13, 14)*.

11   An echo this time, maybe, of a famous lyric by Marlowe (1564-93):

Come live with me, and be my love,
And we will all the pleasures prove,
That valleys, groves, hills and fields,
Woods or steepy mountain yields.

The Little Black Boy

The Society for the Abolition of the Slave Trade was formed in 1787, but at the time that this poem was written the actual abolition was still nearly twenty years away (1806) and the final abolition of slavery within the Empire did not occur until after Blake's death; the act was passed in 1833 and came into effect the following year freeing 770 000 slaves.

In the first verse the poet appears to accept the conventional associations of *white* and *light* with virtue, and *black* with evil, even while claiming that the black boy is nevertheless as virtuous as his white brother. The black boy's skin, however, is better able to endure the heat of the sun, to which the hot *beams* of God's love are compared, and he talks of the need to shelter the weaker white boy until he too can endure the *heat* of God's love. What re-evaluation does this force on the reader?

1   **southern wild** Africa.

16 **cloud** The dark-skinned body which provides protection from the sun.

19 **grove** The comparison is between the dark shade of the *grove* of trees which provides protection and the dark body (as in 16).

26-7 The second illustration shows the small white boy leaning against the knees of God, who is seated, while the black boy stands behind, stroking the white boy's hair. God is shown as a shepherd with a bright, sun-like halo.

The Voice of the Ancient Bard

This was probably the last of the *Songs of Innocence* to be written (it was written in a different script) and was later sometimes placed in *Experience*. When placed in, or at the end of, *Innocence*, as it was in seven of the last eight copies, it offers a note of hope, but with an awareness of the problems of the world of experience that have to be overcome (its optimistic tone was perhaps prompted by the early stages of the French Revolution before the Terror). When placed at, or near the end of, *Experience*, it offers a counterpoise to the more gloomy mood of *Introduction* and *Earth's Answer*. Nevertheless, does the fact that the poet's role is now that of the *Bard* (a figure rather like an Old Testament prophet), rather than the innocent *Piper*, suggest that his view of the world has changed?

2 **opening** The beginning of morning; or morning that reveals? Compare with *Earth's Answer* 13-20 (see p.28).

4 **reason** Not the common sense of *A Little Boy Lost* 15, but the rationalism that in Blake's view led to *clouds* of confusion.

9-11   Is there any reason to be found in the meaning for the irregularity
        of the rhythm here?
10   **care** Compare the feelings of Ona's father in *A Little Girl Lost*
        32-4 (p. 43).
11   Is it reasonable to take this as a commentary on many of the adult
        figures in *Experience*?

The Echoing Green

Note how the shortness of the lines brings about a rapid recurrence
of the rhyming sounds. Note also the lightness of the rhythm in
which unstressed syllables regularly come in pairs. What effect do
these devices have on the mood of the poem?

Does the simple happiness described here seem childish? It is
shared by the *old folk*, and the relationship between children and
parents is seen in terms of nature (*Like birds in their nest*). As with *The
Shepherd* the values underlying the poem only become fully apparent through comparison and contrast with other poems.

30   **darkening** Just as the children in *Nurse's Song* (*Innocence*) are
        allowed to play *till the light fades away*, so these children have been
        allowed to enjoy their day to the very end without restriction. Does
        darkening hint at anything more sinister, or merely indicate a quiet
        ending to the day?

Nurse's Song

In what ways are the moods of the adults (both poet and nurse)
related to that of the children? If you are in doubt make a comparison with *The Echoing Green* in which the relationship is similar.

What do the following contribute to the mood:
            the lightly tripping rhythm (e.g. When the VOIces of
            CHILdren are HEARD on the GREEN);
            the internal rhymes (e.g. *rest* and *breast* in 3);
            the alliteration in line 15?

What does the echoing of line 7 in line 13 suggest about the way in which the Nurse gives way to the children?

Look at the words used in the description of nature here. Does the lack of individual detail make the poem rather colourless? Does it help to convey the sense of innocence unaffected by particular experiences at particular places and times?

Compare the last line of the last verse with the last lines of the earlier verses. Do you think it should have three stresses, giving it a feel of heavy finality, or just two to maintain the sense of lightness? If it is assumed that *echoed* has three syllables (so that *-ed* rhymes with *bed*), what is the effect of the poem ending on two unstressed syllables?

As well as the obvious contrast with *Nurse's Song* in *Experience* (p. 31) look at *The Garden of Love* (p.36).

Holy Thursday

From 1782 onwards there was an annual service in St Paul's Cathedral for the children of London's charity schools on the first Thursday in May, which may have been attended by as many as 6000 children. The illustration shows the children led by a beadle (parish supervisor) *walking two and two* in crocodiles across the top and bottom of the page (in a very different pattern to that in *The Echoing Green*, where old and young are shown mingling without constraint).

It is possible to read the poem as a description of innocence or as an ironic attack on the attitudes that make the charity schools necessary (e.g. *lambs* (7) may simply refer to the innocence of the children or to the fact that they are the sacrificial victims of an uncaring society). Is it necessary to choose between these readings or can they co-exist? Before reaching a conclusion see Approaches p. 116.

> 2 **red and blue and green** The uniforms of their different schools.
> 3 **wands as white as snow** Are the *wands* to be seen as signs of the beadles' office which is performed with purity (*white*ness) of motive, or as a means of punishment to curb the natural warmth of

youthful desire with the *snowy* frigidity of old age (the beadles are *Grey* headed)?

5 **flowers** The children; does the fact that the flowers come from a *town* give the image greater meaning?

5-6 The echoes here of Christ's compassionate feeding of the five thousand support a reading of the poem free from irony: *And he commanded the multitude to sit down on the grass* (*Matthew 14, 19*) and *he commanded them to make them all sit down by companies upon the green grass* (*Mark 6, 39*).

9 **mighty wind** As well as suggesting the physical power of their singing, this perhaps suggests its spiritual power by echoing the description of the first coming of the Holy Spirit on the apostles: *there came a sound from heaven as of a rushing mighty wind* (*Acts 2, 2*).

11 **Beneath** The *wise guardians of the poor* may be literally sitting *beneath* the children if special staging has been erected for the occasion, but could *beneath* be taken in a moral sense? Are the *wise guardians* earthbound in a way that the children whose song rises to heaven are not? If so, is it ironic to talk of *wise guardians?*

12 This line may sound rather sentimental, but seems less so when it is recognized as a reference to *Hebrews 13, 2: Be not forgetful to entertain strangers: for thereby some have entertained angels unawares*, which is itself a reference back to the visits of angels in the form of men to Abraham (*Genesis 18, 3*) and to Lot (*Genesis 19, 2*). What implication does the Biblical echo have both for the reader's opinion of the children and for his future treatment of them?

The Divine Image

When Milton talks of the *human face divine* (*Paradise Lost 3, 44*) he means that man is made in God's image, but Blake adapts Milton's words, believing that God is to be found in man. He expresses it with great clarity in *The Everlasting Gospel* when he makes God say to Jesus:

Thou art a Man; God is no more;
Thy own humanity learn to adore.

In the light of this, what would appear to be the *divine image* in this poem?

In what ways do the patterns in the verse (e.g. repetition, antithesis, rhyme or near-rhyme) help to emphasise Blake's message?
 The contrary poem is *The Human Abstract*.

12 **dress** Body.
13 **clime** Country.
17 **must** A command, or a statement of what must inevitably happen in an ideal world of innocence, or both?
18 Blake emphasises the divinity of *all* mankind by echoing the third collect (prayer) for Good Friday: *O merciful God, who hast made all men, and hatest nothing that thou hast made* . . . *Have mercy upon all Jews, Turks, Infidels, and Hereticks.*

The Chimney-Sweeper

One problem posed by this poem is why it should be a song of innocence when it is so clearly set in the world of harsh experience. An answer is suggested if you consider that the speaker in the poem is not Blake himself. Look at the last line: what difference is there between the attitude of the chimney sweep and what we may safely presume to be Blake's attitude on the evidence of the companion piece in *Experience?*
 Boys were to all intents and purposes sold at about the age of five or six to master sweeps. They suffered from a variety of diseases of the eyes and lungs and often from cancer of the scrotum; early death was common.

3 **weep** Means (s)weep, but also suggests the boy's suffering.
6 **like a lamb's back** Compare the linking of child and lamb in *The Lamb*. What does it suggest about Tom?
9 **he was quiet** In *The Lamb* child and lamb are linked to the child Jesus who is the Lamb of God. Here Tom is compared to a lamb who is quiet before his shearers. Compare this to the following passage from the Old Testament which has traditionally been interpreted

by Christians as referring to the suffering of Jesus: *He was oppressed, and he was afflicted, yet he opened not his mouth: he is brought as a lamb to the slaughter, and as a sheep before her shearers is dumb, so he openeth not his mouth* (*Isaiah* 53, 7). If you find this association puzzling see the notes on *The Lamb* (p. 53) and in Approaches (pp. 92-3).

12   **coffins of black** The constriction of the dark chimney; or the sooty life-denying circumstances of the sweepers; or even their bodies, if we accept the idea that the spirit undergoes a kind of death when it is clothed in the 'grave' of the body (see Approaches p.108).

17   **bags** of soot.

19   **if he'd be a good boy** Do you find the tone of this patronizing or restrictive? Is the effect ironic? On the evidence of the last line how do the sweeps themselves react to the words?

20   **want** Lack.

24   Is the tone of this ironic, or does the irony lie in the gap between the sweep's feelings and Blake's own attitude?

A Cradle Song

This poem is on two pages. The first is decorated with an abstract pattern, but softly tinted with *moony beams* (4); for a comparable linking of innocent and protected sleep with the light of the moon see *The Little Girl Lost* 31-2. The second page shows the mother watching over her child, whose pillow forms what looks like a halo round its head; this reinforces the ideas of 21-4.

4   **By** Revealed by; or, accompanied by.

12   **beguiles** Charm away (the long hours of the night); the *s* has been added for the sake of the rhyme, as in the next verse.

15   The *moans* are the child's, but the *sweeter smiles* are presumably the mother's.

20   Are the tears of the protective mother compatible with Blake's idea of innocence? Compare *On Another's Sorrow* 9-12 and 20.

22   **image** of the Christ child.

The Little Boy Lost and
The Little Boy Found

(Avoid confusion with *A Little Boy Lost*.)

These two poems should be taken in conjunction. In the first of the pair the *father* that the boy addresses is indeed shown in the illustration as a *vapour*, an insubstantial, will o' the wisp shape that leads the child astray, the *wand'ring light* of the second poem. (Milton compares Satan when he is leading Eve into temptation with *A wandering fire Compact of unctuous vapour*, which *misleads the amazed night-wanderer from his way* - Paradise Lost 9, 633-45). In contrast with this abstract and uncommunicative father (or god?) is the figure of God in human form who rescues the boy in the second poem. Two comments from Blake will serve to throw light on this:

God only acts and is in existing beings or men (*Marriage of Heaven and Hell*).

Think of a white cloud as being holy, you cannot love it; but think of a holy man within the cloud, love springs up in your thoughts, for to think of holiness distinct from man is impossible to the affections (a note on Swedenborg's *Divine Love* in which the latter comments on the puzzlement of primitive peoples at the suggestion that God exists in the midst of a cloud and on their inability to envisage God in any other form than human). See also Approaches p.123.

Night

This poem presents a picture of security in which guardian angels *pour blessing* on every form of life and if their protection fails then they escort the spirits of the dead to an ideal world such as Isaiah describes in a passage often taken to foretell the nature of Christ's kingdom: *The wolf also shall dwell with the lamb, and the leopard shall lie down with the kid; and the calf and the young lion and the fatling together; and a little child shall lead them* (Isaiah 11, 6).

6 **bower** A poetic term for a dwelling place or a shady recess surrounded by plants; the comparison of the moon to a flower suggests the latter meaning.

9 **Farewell** This may simply refer to the loss of the colour green with the coming of night, or it may look forward to the departure for other *worlds* referred to in 32.

26 **stand and weep** Is there a hint of ineffectiveness as well as pity here?

27 **thirst** A thirst for blood; are the angels trying to combat the bloodlust of the beasts of prey, as well as trying to keep the beasts themselves at a distance?

37 **his** Presumably *Christ's* in view of 43.

37-9 Both *wrath* and *sickness* are the subjects of *Is driven away*. What patterning of language is made possible by this? Does the pattern reinforce the meaning?

40 **immortal day** In the *new world* of Heaven there is neither darkness nor death.

41-2 See the quotation from *Isaiah* given in the headnote.

43 **him who bore thy name** Jesus Christ is the *Lamb* of God (compare the second verse of *The Lamb*, p. 7).

44 **Graze** Eat grass; what is the significance of this?

45 **life's river** Water is a powerful religious symbol: not only is it essential for life, but also for cleansing and healing. The passing of the Jews through the Red Sea, thus escaping from slavery and setting out for the Promised Land, is seen as *figuring . . . holy Baptism* (*Book of Common Prayer*) in which the sinner is not only washed free of sin, but dies to sin beneath the water and is raised to a new and sinless life. Compare also Christian in Bunyan's *Pilgrim's Progress* who passes through the river of death to new life in Heaven. Ezekiel has a vision of a holy river (47, 1-12) which is echoed in *Revelation 22, 1-2: And he shewed me a pure river of water of life, clear as crystal, proceeding out of the throne of God and of the Lamb . . . and on either side of the river was the tree of life.*

Songs of Experience

Introduction

The first two poems of *Experience* should be read together. The tone and content of *Earth's Answer*, coupled with a direct response to the poetry, provide the best guide to tackling the difficulties of *Introduction*.

Two of the terms here need explanation straightaway. The *bard* is a prophetic figure who not only sees the future, but who also speaks out against the wrongs of the present. The *Word* is a more complex term; it is associated with the creative power of God (each stage of creation in *Genesis* is introduced with the words: *And God said*); it is also the message of God as spoken through the prophets (Old Testament prophecy is often introduced with such words as: *Thus saith the Lord*, or: *The word of the Lord came unto me, saying*); these two ideas are then combined when St John uses the term in the opening chapter of his gospel to speak of Jesus who, as God made man, embodies both the creative power of God and his message.

The interpretation of this poem provokes considerable disagreement. The initial problems arise from the lack of clarity in Blake's original punctuation and grammatical structure. It is not clear whether it is the *Holy Word* or the *lapsèd soul* that *might control The starry pole*, and neither is it clear whether it is the *bard* or the *Holy Word* who speaks the third and fourth stanzas.

The *starry pole* is Milton's term for the night sky as seen by Adam and Eve before the Fall, but stars are associated elsewhere in Blake with monarchy and war and also with the cold rationalism of Newton's 'single vision' (see Approaches p.98); alternatively *starry pole* might refer to the destiny of man, supposedly governed by the stars. If it is the *Holy Word* that might control the *starry pole* in any of the suggested meanings then the question arises as to why it doesn't. Is the *Word* to be taken as the cruel creative force of *Earth's Answer* (*Selfish father of men*) who comes down to judge Adam and Eve after they have been disobedient (he walks among the trees and weeps in the evening breeze just as the Lord God in *Genesis* walks in the garden in the cool of the day)? In that case are we to assume that the *Word* could help men but won't? If on the other hand the *Word* is Jesus, God the Son, as Milton suggests in *Paradise Lost*, then is there a hint of hope? In the latter case *weeping* might be evidence of sympathy rather than ineffectiveness.

If it is the *lapsèd* [morally fallen] *soul . . . That might control The starry pole* then there is a much stronger ground for hope. Blake might be suggesting that, despite the gloomy picture the following poems paint, humanity could bring back an era of renewed light.

The next problem is the identity of the speaker of the third and fourth stanzas. The opening words of stanza three echo various passages of denunciation in the Old Testament. Moses' summary in *Deuteronomy 32,1* of the faults of the Jews opens with the words *Hear O earth* and is immediately followed by God's judgment which allows him to see the Promised Land, but not to reach it *because ye trespassed against me*; likewise Jeremiah's condemnation of the kings of Judah is followed by the words: *O earth, earth, earth, hear the word of the Lord.* Such associations suggest a harsh Urizen-like figure as the speaker (see Approaches p.94), but the plea to return and the promise of new light strike a more optimistic note like that of the words of *Isaiah* 60,1 which herald a new era of peace: *Arise, shine; for thy light is come, and the glory of the Lord is risen upon thee. For, behold, the darkness shall cover the earth, and gross darkness the people: but the Lord shall arise upon thee, and his glory shall be seen upon thee.* The words of the fourth stanza, however, suggest a renewal of a rather querulous objection to Earth's behaviour, not least in the repetition in the second line. If the *starry floor* represents the limitations of a rational Newtonian universe and the *wat'ry shore* is an image of the material world of time and space in which the soul is trapped (see Approaches p.108), then what is offered the Earth *till the break of day* is very far from satisfactory in Blake's terms and the bitter reply of Earth in the next poem is fully understandable. Are we then to see the speaker as hypocritical or inconsistent in what he offers?

An alternative is that the *bard* is the speaker. In that case the same questions still apply as to the nature of the message and of the speaker. Is the *bard* truly inspired with a vision of new hope, or has his inspiration become corrupted like that of the priests who are *binding with briars my joys and desires* (p. 36)?

2 **present, past and future** Is the bard's vision not bound by the limitations of time, or is he in fact a false prophet whose limited vision actually imposes such divisions?

5 **ancient trees** The trees of the Garden of Eden were young at the time. Are these the trees of a Druidical place of worship and sacrifice where the bard prophesies? (See note on *Earth's Answer* – p. 69) (Blake puts a full stop after *trees*.)

6 **lapsèd** Two syllables.

7 **weeping** Does this suggest hypocrisy, ineffectiveness, or sympathy (as in Jesus weeping over Jerusalem)?

8 **That might control** Earth (humanity) can even now make a fresh start, or the *Holy Word* could *control* if it wanted to, but won't?

9 **starry pole** See headnote.

10 **fallen, fallen** Does the first *fallen* describe the light or the condition of the one who might control it (either the *Holy Word* or the *lapsèd soul*)? (There is no comma after the first *fallen* in the original.) Is *fallen light* the dark condition of the world after the Fall, or Lucifer (whose name means 'light-bearer'), the arch rebel against a tyrannical God?

11-20 The inverted commas are editorial.

15 **slumberous mass** The material world in which the soul is trapped and not truly awake?

Earth's Answer

Earth with all its natural growth, life and potential for love is pictured as a woman *Prisoned* by the *Selfish father of men*. Is it helpful to see the Urizen-like figure of a jealous god with his reason and restrictions (see Approaches p. 94) as representing an essentially 'masculine' attitude to life which has little time for a 'feminine' expression of, and fulfilment of, earthly love and feelings?

4 **Stony dread** Does *Stony* merely imply lack of life, or is there a hint of Medusa here, whose snaky hair turned those who saw it to stone?

5 **locks** hair.

6 This line may just refer to the soul entrapped in the physical world

of time and space, although there is possibly a reference to Andromeda who was tied on a rock on the sea-shore by her father to
propitiate an angry sea monster.

7 **Starry jealousy** *I the Lord thy God am a jealous God* (from the Ten
Commandments, e.g. *Exodus 20, 5*).

10 **father of the ancient men** If *ancient men* is a reference to the Druids
who practised human sacrifice, then the implication could be that
God demands cruel sacrifices (like Andromeda's father and other
fathers in these poems).

13-15 Is *delight* or *virgins* the subject of *bear*? Does *bear* mean 'endure', or
'carry with one', or 'give birth to'? *Chained in night* can presumably
apply to both *delight* and *virgins*. Despite these alternatives a
comparison with *Ah! Sunflower* suggests that the likely meaning is
that the *virgins* cannot experience joy while *chained in night*, but
long for the *sweet golden clime* (p. 35); in other words, as the next
stanza suggests, creative fulfilment is not possible under the dark
restrictions of a material world governed by the harsh laws of a
jealous god. Compare also the destructive effect of the worm's *dark
secret love* in *The Sick Rose* (p. 31).

21 **chain** The restrictions of a life-denying moral code; the physical
body into which the soul 'dies' at birth (See Approaches p. 108);
the rationality of a *single vision* that cramps the creative imagination
of love. Are these interpretations compatible, or even linked?

The Clod and the Pebble

There is disagreement as to how this song should be interpreted.
Some point to the indignity of the Clod's position *Trodden with the
cattle's feet* and argue that Blake's sympathies lie with the Pebble
whose words are described as *meet* (fitting). Furthermore Hell is
presented as an attractive place of uninhibited energy in *The
Marriage of Heaven and Hell* (see Approaches pp. 123-4). *Meet*, however, could well be ironic, and others would argue that the self-
sacrificing love of the Clod is clearly preferable to the hard selfishness of the Pebble surrounded by the water that is often a symbol of
materialism in Blake. It is possible to support this view by referring
to Blake's poem *The Book of Thel* (etched in 1789) in which a Clod

of Clay speaks and admits it is the *meanest thing*, but goes on to say:

> ... he that loves the lowly, pours his oil upon my head,
> And kisses me, and binds his nuptial bands around my breast
> And says: 'Thou mother of my children, I have loved thee
> And I have given thee a crown that none can take away.'

Your own verdict will depend on whether you see the third verse as:
  a) a statement that the self should not be bound down by an inhibiting external morality;
  b) a shameless assertion of selfish desires;
  c) a warning of how the ideal love of the first verse may degenerate into a hypocritical disguise for the real motives described by the Pebble.
In support of c) you might compare the supposed virtue implied by the ironic title *Christian Forbearance* for a draft of *A Poison Tree*, when in fact that *forbearance* was only a disguise for hate.

8   **metres** The rhythmical lines of the next verse.

Holy Thursday

For an account of Holy Thursday see the notes on the contrary poem in *Innocence*. What impact do the many short, end-stopped lines have?

1   **holy** What light does this throw on the values that might otherwise be thought to be assumed in the title? Does it suggest a different approach to that in the previous poem of this title?
4   **usurous** Usury, the receiving of interest on loans of money, is forbidden in the Old Testament. By Blake's time the term was used in particular for charging illegal or excessive interest. What kind of interest, financial or otherwise, might those responsible for feeding the children of the charity schools obtain? (The poet Coleridge spoke of the uniformed crocodiles of charity children as *walking advertisements*.) Alternatively, perhaps the schools have been founded with the profits of usury.
8   In what sense is this line ironic and in what sense is it true? Consider the rest of the poem before reaching your conclusion.

The Chimney-Sweeper

Unlike the boy in the contrary poem this sweep has no illusions; does this make the poem more, or less, effective? Which seems preferable: the ignorance of innocence or the knowledge of experience?

2 **weep** Sweep, the call for work of the boy going through the streets, but also the tearful *notes of woe*.

4-12 These lines are the words of the boy in reply to the question in 3.

4 What does the activity of the parents suggest about Blake's attitude to the church as well as to the parents? Compare the ironic use of *heaven* in line 12.

5 **Because** What does this suggest about the parental attitude to the natural exuberance of childhood? In an earlier draft the poem began at this point. What effect on the impact and clarity of the poem does the addition of the first stanza have?

9-10 The fact that the child is still capable of happiness is used by the parents to justify their exploitation of him. Is there evidence of hypocrisy here?

11-12 What makes possible the *heaven* of the authorities of Church and State?

Nurse's Song

There is only one speaker in this poem. Refer back to *Nurse's Song* in *Innocence* (p. 17) and consider what is lost as a result.

Compare line 2 with line 2 of the earlier poem; what is the effect of the alterations?

The greenness and paleness of the Nurse's face (4) may be indicative of her frustration and lack of fulfilment. If this is so, do you think that the second verse is simply a sad statement that the children's youth and innocence (*Your spring and your day*) have now passed away, or is there a hint of jealousy, a wish that the children should not enjoy the youth that she has already lost? Consider the implications of *wasted* in line 7. (It may help to consider the illustration of this poem which shows a boy submitting to having his hair combed by his nurse while a girl is slumped apathetically waiting on the ground. Behind is a doorway surrounded with bunches of grapes and vine leaves, suggesting perhaps the pleasures of life that still await the young once they leave the domination of the nurse. See p. 141.)

What do *night* and *disguise* suggest about the loss of innocence? You may find it helpful to return to this question after looking at the next poem, *The Sick Rose*, in which the *worm* is *invisible* and *flies in the night*.

The Sick Rose

The illustration shows the worm entering the rose while another figure (the life of the rose?) leaves. In addition in the top left-hand corner a caterpillar eats one of the leaves and lower down on the very thorny branches are two figures in what seem to be postures of despair. (See p. 142.) These further details offer a hint of how to read the poem since Blake regards the caterpillar as a symbol of destruction just as it is in the Bible (e.g. *and that which the cankerworm hath left hath the caterpillar eaten, Joel 1, 4*). Elsewhere he associates it with the priesthood and this, taken in conjunction with the thorns, might lead us to *The Garden of Love* where the priests were *binding . . . my joys and desires* with the *briars* of a repressive moral code.

Any specific interpretation of this poem will limit its power, but the rose is a traditional symbol of love and female beauty, while the worm is a symbol of male sexuality; the love in this poem, however, is *secret* and corrupting and so the worm becomes the cankerworm that destroys. Compare with:

> She never told her love,
> But let concealment, like a worm i' the bud,
> Feed on her damask [i.e. rose-coloured] cheek.
> *(Twelfth Night II, iv)*

A comparison with *The Blossom* (p. 7) will also highlight the lack of openness and the consequent loss of shared, natural, innocent emotion. The world of experience with its restrictive moral code promotes secrecy and selfish possessiveness. What qualities does the poem suggest are corrupted in this world?

Benjamin Britten's setting of this poem in the section of his *Serenade* entitled *Elegy* is one of the most beautiful of Blake settings, the plaintive introduction on horn and strings bringing out well the sense of secrecy and melancholy (see p. 132).

2-8   What is the effect of explaining the statement of the opening line in a single sentence that presses on to the very end of the poem? (Britten's setting brings out well the sense of unbroken movement to an inevitable conclusion.)

8   What emphasis is created by the slight alteration to the normal word-order here?

The Fly

A crucial question is whether we are to take the speaker of this poem as expressing Blake's own views. If he is, then the conclusion of the poem can be taken as a philosophical acceptance of death whenever it comes. There are, however, two possible reasons for doubting this. The first is the reference to the *blind hand*, since this suggests a casual and uncaring divinity very different from the *human form divine* of *Mercy, Pity, Peace and Love* that Blake takes to be the *Divine Image*. The second is the assumption that the fly is of no importance except as a reminder that the speaker too will be killed one day when touched by *some blind hand*. Blake's own view, however, is that *Everything that lives is Holy* and that every fly *has a heart like thee, a brain open to heaven and hell Withinside wondrous and expansive* (*Milton* Book 1). If the speaker's views are not Blake's, but limited by the world of experience, then you need to decide in what way the conclusions of the poem are inadequate. Is thought the *only* quality of a fully lived life? Is the fatalism of the last stanza an excuse for lack of thought in general, or an excuse for the lack of thought that led to the killing of the fly?

The illustration of this poem appears irrelevant at first sight; a boy is being taught to walk by his mother and a girl is playing by herself with a shuttlecock. (See p. 143.) It could be argued, however, that both children reveal the inhibiting nature of education in the world of experience. The boy is quite large and should be able to walk already, but has both his mother and the curving arch of a very dead-looking branch bending oppressively over him, and the girl looks sexually mature, but is reduced to playing a children's game and furthermore has to play by herself although the game needs two players. Children brought up in this way may well do nothing more than *dance And drink and sing* until they die.

Do the short nursery-rhyme-like lines suggest the movement of the fly? Do they hint at the triteness of the speaker's thoughts?

2 **summer's play** Not merely the flight of the fly, but its very life, on the evidence of a stanza that Blake originally wrote to follow this first one:

> The cut worm
> Forgives the plough
> And dies in peace
> And so do thou.

15 **want** lack.

The Angel

Compare with *My Pretty Rose Tree* and *The Lily* for the treatment of love.

Is the poem about the rejection of a guardian angel, or of a lover? The last stanza may help you to decide.

2 **maiden** In what way are the conventional associations of this word changed by the end of the poem?

4 A difficult line! Is the *woe* of the next stanza perhaps *witless* because it is insincere and finally self-defeating (see last stanza)? This foolish *woe* prevents her being *beguiled* by the angel's love, but was

this love really deceitful, or is that only a *self*-deceiving argument used by the girl to keep true love at arm's length (as she does quite literally in the illustration)?

5-8 If you are in doubt as to the nature of her tears make a comparison with the second stanza of *A Poison Tree* (p. 40).

8 **heart's delight** Her true feelings of love.

12 **shields and spears** The means for both defence and assault in the war of the sexes? or the *thorns* of false modesty and shame?

16 Literally old, or just an 'old maid' in her attitudes?

The Tiger

For a detailed discussion of this poem see the first section of Approaches (p. 90-102). Benjamin Britten's setting of this poem in *Songs and Proverbs of William Blake* gives a fiercely exhilarating rendering of the powerful rhythm of this poem. (See p. 132.)

4 **frame** create.

7 **aspire** Both *rise up* and *have a burning ambition*.

9 **shoulder** The implication is that strength as well as *art* (skill) are needed to create the tiger.

12 In an earlier draft this line was followed by the words *Could fetch it from the furnace deep?* Is there a loss of clarity in the final version? Does the poem gain anything in impact from the revision?

20 **lamb** The original has a capital letter here, perhaps a reminder of Jesus, the Lamb of God, who went to his death in a most untigerish manner (although he sometimes showed the revolutionary fire of the tiger: *I came not to send peace, but a sword - Matthew 10, 34*). Does Blake expect the reader to answer his rhetorical question in this line, or has he already made his point that both extremes are to be found in creation?

24 Note the change of wording from 4.

My Pretty Rose Tree

This was etched on the same page as *Ah! Sunflower* and *The Lily*.

2   More beautiful than any flower of May.
8   **my only delight** What makes it ironic that where he might have expected *delight* he only receives *thorns*? What appears to be the 'moral'? (Compare the last line of *The Garden of Love*.)

Ah! Sunflower

The Roman poet Ovid tells in *Metamorphoses* how the virgin Clytie pined away for love of the sun-god and was turned into a flower which followed the movement of the sun. The sunflower is rooted in earth, but yearns to reach that *sweet golden clime*. *Clime* literally means *country*, but there is perhaps a suggestion also of the Golden Age.

There is no main verb; in other words the poem makes no statement. Does this give the poem a timeless quality, or make it a yearning exclamation?

What does the contrast between the warmth of the sunny *golden clime* and the *snow* that shrouds the virgin suggest about the desires of the youth and the virgin? Whether you interpret the poem as optimistic or only yearning will depend on the meaning you attribute to *aspire*: does it mean 'desperately desire to go' or 'successfully reach up to'? Is the last line merely a reminder of the sunflower's longing, or an indication that the sunflower's continued longing is evidence of its unfulfilled desire?

The Lily

The white lily is traditionally a symbol of purity. Here it is shown as putting forth none of the defences against love that the rose and even the sheep (elsewhere a symbol of innocence) regard as necessary. What does this imply about Blake's view of love? Is this a song of experience? If so, does it suggest a possible reconciliation of the contraries of innocence and experience, in which an acceptance of sexual love can co-exist with innocence? (In considering these questions bear in mind the sequence of attitudes to love portrayed in the three poems on the same page – *My Pretty Rose Tree, Ah! Sunflower, The Lily.*)

The Garden of Love

This is the contrary poem of *The Echoing Green* (see 4). The illustration shows a priest holding a book and kneeling with two young people behind him who are presumably learning from him.

What is implied about love if its garden is also the place of childhood play? What alternative view of love is the Church presented as having?

   6   **Thou shalt not** The opening words of six of the Ten Command-
        ments; Blake presumably also has in mind these words about the
        need to drive home God's laws: *And ye shall teach* [God's laws to]
        *your children, speaking of them when thou sittest in thine house, and
        when thou walkest by the way, when thou liest down, and when thou
        risest up. And thou shalt write them upon the door posts of thine house,
        and upon thy gates* (*Deuteronomy 11, 19-20*).

  11 **black gowns** In the original draft Blake wrote *gounds*, thus making
        an internal rhyme with *rounds*, just as there is between *briars* and
        desires in the next line. (*Gounds* was the Cockney pronunciation –
        it is also used by Jo in Dickens's *Bleak House*.) Are the gowns *black*
        figuratively as well as literally?

11-12 What is the effect of the contrast between the light rhythm in these
        last two lines and their subject matter? (It is the same rhythm as in
        The Echoing Green.)

The Little Vagabond

Compare the tone in this and the two *Chimney-Sweeper* poems. Is this a voice of complete or partial experience, of naïvety or of irony?

The criticism of the church is from a different angle from that in *The Garden of Love*, but again attacks its joylessness. The poem was thought sufficiently subversive to be suppressed when the *Songs* were first published in 1839.

4   **usage** treatment.

6   **regale** entertain.

11   **modest dame Lurch** Presumably the school mistress, or possibly a mother, who has failed to show true love to her children, 'leaving them in the lurch'; for the overtones of *modest* compare Blake's use of the word in *The Lily* (p. 36).

12   **bandy** With curving legs (a typical symptom of rickets, which was caused by lack of sunlight).

       fasting, nor birch Methods of punishment.

15   **the barrel** i.e. ale.

13-16 The last verse is suggestive of the story of the Prodigal Son who is welcomed home with *both drink and apparel* (clothing), in contrast to the welcome that the church offers the vagabond. (Blake's engraving for this poem shows a father-like figure, surrounded by a large halo, embracing a kneeling youth, who could be the Prodigal Son. A group, perhaps a family, are shown underneath warming themselves at a large fire.)

London

For a discussion of this complex poem see Approaches pp. 105-8.

1   **chartered** A charter can mean a number of different things, several of which deserve consideration:

     a) the written acceptance of rights or granting of privileges (as in Magna Carta);

     b) the royal document founding a city or borough;

     c) conveyancing documents in the purchase of land;

     d) a contract of hire.

Clearly it depends on your viewpoint as to whether the description seems a flattering one or not. The word suggesting the proud independence of a great city could also be taken to mean that the very river itself is so far from being *life's river* (*Night* 45 pp. 23-4) that it is sold; nothing is free in either sense of the word.

3   **mark** This could mean either *notice* or *make a mark*. See Approaches for a discussion of the implications of this ambiguity (pp. 107-8).

7   **ban** Curse (i.e. a swear-word); this is presumably what Blake would have heard in the streets, but the alternative meaning of a formal prohibition made by either church or state is worth considering. In view of the final stanza is it unreasonable to suggest a link with marriage banns (sometimes spelt with one *n* in the eighteenth century, but usually in the plural)?

8   **manacles** Literally handcuffs, and so imprisoning restraints. Are they only *forged* in the minds of the oppressors, or in those of the oppressed as well?

9   **cry** *weep, weep* (*The Chimney-Sweeper, Experience*).

10   **appalls** Horrifies; casts a funeral pall over (a pall was a cloth – normally black – to cover a coffin or hearse: hence the church *black'ning* with the pall of death or of soot). Is the literal meaning of *to turn pale* irrelevant?

11   **hapless** Unfortunate. Is this adjective unexpected? What does it imply about Blake's attitude to the ordinary soldier?

14   **harlot's** prostitute's.

15-16   **Blasts; blights** Infects and ruins; venereal disease can be passed on to both marriage partner and child, but is this all that this final stanza implies? Compare Blake's attitude in *My Pretty Rose Tree* or in this proverb from *The Marriage of Heaven and Hell*: *brothels* [are built] *with bricks of religion*.

The Human Abstract

This is the contrary poem to *The Divine Image*. *Abstract* suggests a lack of real substance by comparison with *Image*; perhaps that the *Mercy, Pity, Peace and Love* of *The Divine Image* (p. 19) can be merely ideas, lacking real value (1-6). Alternatively *Abstract* could mean summary, in which case the poem is offered as a gloomy summary of human nature. The illustration shows an old man tied down by ropes at the foot of a bare tree.

1-2   Is this merely saying that pity, although apparently a virtue, is only possible in an unfair world, or is it suggesting that the act of pitying in itself makes its recipients poor by placing them under an obligation?

5   **Peace** In writing of a *peace* based on fear of one another Blake was probably not thinking in terms of an international balance of power, but of the Social Contract in which members of society surrender certain freedoms in exchange for the mutual protection of society's laws (see Approaches p. 112).

9   **holy** Fear can be *holy* (e.g. *The fear of the Lord is the beginning of wisdom*, *Psalm 111, 10*). What reasons are there for supposing that Blake is either ironic or merely using the word to suggest the oppressive way in which he thinks of church teaching influencing people? (Compare *The Garden of Love*.) Consider also the meaning of *Humility* in 11.

10   **waters the ground** Compare the circumstances and consequences of the growth of this tree and that in *A Poison Tree*.

14   **Mystery** This can mean a religious truth made known by divine revelation and beyond human understanding, or a sacrament of the church, but Blake uses the image of the tree of Mystery to suggest religious error. At the same time in 17 and 18 he draws on the idea of the tree of knowledge of good and evil which led to the Fall of Adam and Eve (see also note on *A Poison Tree* p.81).

15   **caterpillar and fly** What does Blake imply about those who feed on false religion? (See note on *The Sick Rose* p. 72.)

19   **raven** A bird of ill-omen and death.

21-4   As well as the story of Adam and Eve, Blake has perhaps drawn on the story of the upas tree which supposedly poisoned every living thing within a wide radius. No evidence, of course, had been found of a tree having such an effect, but according to Blake the reason for this is that the tree is not to be found in *Nature*, but in the human mind.

Infant Sorrow

The contrary poem of *Infant Joy*. In the illustration the mother is leaning down over the infant who is leaning back and waving its arms in protest.

1   Is the initial behaviour of the parents the reason for the difference in the response of the infants in the two poems?
3   **piping** The crying of the baby? In what way does this *piping* differ from that in the *Introduction* of *Innocence*?
4   **a fiend** What does fiend suggest about the child's character and energy? Is it better to *struggle* or to *sulk*?
     hid in a cloud Elsewhere Blake uses the *cloud* as a symbol of the body (e.g. *The Little Black Boy* 23, pp. 14-15). Does the *cloud* suggest something of the restriction of the *swaddling bands*?
6   **swaddling bands** Bandage-like strips wound round the limbs of a baby. Is the restriction they represent only physical?
7-8 What change of attitude is there here? How positive is the infant's attitude to its mother? What is implied about its attitude to its father?

A Poison Tree

In manuscript this poem has the title *Christian Forbearance*, an ironic comment on the supposed virtue of restraint that in fact leads to *deceitful wiles*. The poem stands as a psychologically perceptive account of the effect of bottling up anger; note that *fears* play their part in building up destructive hate. Nevertheless *apple* (10) suggests the story of *Paradise Lost*; what if the narrator were God? (See Approaches p.125.) The illustration arguably supports this; it shows the *foe* prostrate beneath a low, heavy branch of the tree.

1-4 What is the effect of these terse, contrasting statements?
4   Note how the double meaning of *grow* introduces the central image suggested by the title.
8   **wiles** Cunning devices.
12   Why is it important that the foe *knew that it was mine*? (What does

the narrator want to happen?) What effect on the pace of the story does the repetition of *And* have at this point?

14 **pole** The sky.

16 Compare Milton's description in *Paradise Lost* (10, 850-2) of Adam after he has disobeyed God and eaten the apple:

```
... On the ground
Outstretched he lay, on the cold ground, and oft
Cursed his creation.
```

A Little Boy Lost

Unlike *The Little Boy Lost* in *Innocence*, this is not followed by a poem of rescue. For a further contrast with the idea of true religion being in terms of humanity rather than *mystery* look at *On Another's Sorrow* (pp. 9-10).

2 **venerates** Looks upon with feelings of reverence and awe.

3-4 Man cannot conceive of anything greater than himself because he has no other experience on which to draw. How does this point of view compare with that of the priest who defends the *most holy mystery*?

7-8 Is this primarily an image of dependence, of innocence or of naturalness?

10 **trembling zeal** Zeal is religious enthusiasm, but what does *trembling* suggest here? Compare with the father's reactions in *A Little Girl Lost* 32 (pp. 42-3).

11 **little** What is the effect of this word here and in 19?

12 Is the tone here factual or ironic?

15 **reason** Common sense.

16 **mystery** A religious truth that cannot be judged by reason alone; for Blake's feelings about *mystery* see 3-4, but also *The Human Abstract* (p.39).

24 **Albion's** Britain's. If the answer to Blake's question is yes, what other examples of 'sacrifice' does he give in *Experience*?

A Little Girl Lost

This is the contrary poem to *The Little Girl Lost* which was originally in *Innocence*. If the earlier poem was partly about sexual experience as the illustrations possibly suggest, then an important part of the contrast is in the parental attitudes. The *age of gold* is an ideal time of innocence, such as that in the Garden of Eden before the Fall, when there were no moral restrictions on love (see Approaches p. 120 for more on the Fall).

1-4   **the future age** What attitude is Blake implying will have changed in *the future age*?

5-9   Compare the *age of gold* with the darkness and cold which is described in *Earth's Answer* as *chaining* the *delight* of the *virgins of youth and morning* (p. 28).

6   **winter's cold** Before the Fall when Adam and Eve were expelled from the Garden of Eden there were no extremes of temperature. What else, however, is implied here about the treatment of love in the ordinary world? Contrast with the *pale virgin shrouded in snow* (*Ah! Sunflower* p. 35).

13-14   Compare the fourth stanza of *Earth's Answer*.

25   **white** Does this suggest purity, sexual coldness, age?

27   What sort of love is this?

28   **holy book** The Bible includes the books of the Law.

30   **Ona** The girl's name, perhaps suggested by analogy with Una in Spenser's *The Fairy Queen*, who is falsely suspected of lechery.

34   **blossoms of my hoary hair** *Hoary* means white like hoar frost, and so suggests both coldness and age here. Are you conscious of an irony, which presumably escapes the father, in the use of *blossoms* to suggest this whiteness?

To Tirzah

This is a much later poem than the others in *Experience* and was only added to the later copies. Tirzah is a figure in Blake's later poems who torments man by binding him down to earthly existence. The escape from this torment, or from the suffering caused by the Fall (see Approaches p. 120) is pictured in the illustration (p. 145), which shows a dying body supported by two women while an old man (the apostle St. Paul or the prophet Elijah?) bends over it with a jug containing perhaps the water of life. On the old man's robe is written *It is Raised a Spiritual Body* from St Paul's teaching about the nature of the resurrection of the dead: *thou sowest not that body that shall be, but bare grain, it may chance of wheat, or of some other grain* [i.e. the seed that you sow is different in form to the plant that it will grow into]: *But God giveth it a body as it hath pleased him, and to every seed his own body . . . So also is the resurrection of the dead . . . It is sown a natural body; it is raised a spiritual body* (I *Corinthians* 15, 37-44).

What kind of solution does the poem offer to the suffering described by Earth, trapped on the *wat'ry shore* (of physical matter), in *Earth's Answer?* Is it a pessimistic or optimistic solution?

2 **consumed with the earth** Death is one of the consequences of the Fall; part of the judgment on Adam was that he would *return unto the ground: for out of it wast thou taken: for dust thou art, and unto dust shalt thou return* (*Genesis* 3, 19).

3 **generation** Mortal existence derived from one's parents, or the act of begetting the next generation, or the mortal world (the meaning Blake seems to give to this word in his later writing)?

4 These words were spoken by Jesus when he was asked by his mother to provide more wine at the wedding in Cana (*John* 2, 4). He appears to be asserting his independence of the mother who has *generated* him, just before he performs the first of his life-enhancing signs. The same words are spoken to Elijah by the widow whose son has died, just before Elijah brings him back to life again (*I Kings* 17, 18). The words are thus doubly appropriate to the theme of rejecting an earthly mother in favour of new life.

5-8 These lines could be taken to summarize the Fall: both the *shame* that Adam and Eve feel, which leads to their covering their nakedness with fig leaves, and their sentence, which means that they must *work and weep: I will greatly multiply thy sorrow and thy conception* and *In the sweat of thy face shalt thou eat bread* (*Genesis* 3).

6 **Blowed** bloomed.

9 Tirzah is only the creator of the physical body.

10   **mould** Compare the description of creation with that in *The Tiger*.

12-13   The four of the five senses that are located in specific parts of the body. Does the use of *bind* and *close* suggest that the senses are a guide to truth? In what way(s) is the *clay* (physical substance of his body) *senseless*?

15   The orthodox Christian view is that on the cross Jesus undergoes the punishment for mankind's sins, but is Blake thinking of death as a punishment or as a release? More important to him is the subsequent resurrection to a spiritual life: *But now is Christ risen from the dead, and become the firstfruits of them that slept. For since by man came death, by man came also the resurrection of the dead* (*I Corinthians 15, 20-21*).

A Divine Image

Although Blake etched this poem, he never included it in a copy of *Experience*. It provides an even more savage contrary poem to *The Divine Image* than the *The Human Abstract*.

Approaches

Introduction

Two things were happening in 1789, one of which went unnoticed by all but a handful of people, the other of which attracted the attention of the whole of Europe and America as well, and yet both were part of a change which two hundred years later still affects the way that we think, feel and organize our societies. In London an engraver, known to few outside a small circle of friends, was making a series of engravings which combined the words of some short poems of his own with pictures designed to frame, decorate and illustrate them. When he had printed them he proceeded to colour them by hand, producing a series of exquisitely produced, hand-made works of art. These apparently simple poems, Blake's *Songs of Innocence*, give one man's highly personal view, not altogether without hope, of a world in which a revolution, not merely of politics but also of feeling, was urgently required. In France a political revolution was actually taking place. Louis XVI, faced with political unrest and a financial crisis, had called together the Estates General, or parliament, which had not met since 1614. In this way he unintentionally began the process of reform, which was soon to become revolution and to sweep away the old privileges of the nobility and king, paving the way for democracy.

Five years later, however, the ideals of the revolution were beginning to look somewhat tarnished. It was true that France had resisted foreign attempts to overthrow the revolution and had declared itself a republic, but following the execution of its king it had also been through the dark days of the Terror, when not only had many aristocrats been sent to the guillotine, but also many of the leaders of the revolution who had been caught up in the subsequent in-fighting. The Terror ended in July 1794 with the death of Robespierre, who had been virtual dictator for a year. By then most English reformers had ceased to regard the French Revolution as a model to follow towards a more democratic society; indeed the war with France and fears of violent revolution had set back the cause of reform in Britain for many years. William Blake, however, had not lost his own personal vision of a world in which freedom of the spirit was to be restored, but by 1794, when he had completed the engraving of a companion collection of poems, *Songs of Experience*, his attack on the abuses which oppress the human spirit had become much more bitter.

It can be seen, therefore, that Blake was a man of his times up to a point, but one who, unlike many, never abandoned his revolutionary vision. This vision of the world was an intensely personal one, as was his poetic style, which means that the reader of his poems has to come to them without pre-conceptions, and be willing to try a series of different approaches which, *taken together*, should lead to a fuller understanding and enjoyment of his undoubted genius.

Different methods of approach

One thing which strikes many readers of *Songs of Innocence and of Experience* is the apparent contrast between the simplicity of some of the *Songs of Innocence,* which perhaps even seem childish and hardly worthy of serious study, and the complexity of other poems which provoke explanations from the critics that may seem to be far-fetched, and that are certainly contradictory at times, as we shall see. *The Lamb* in *Innocence* is a poem of the first type and its companion piece in *Experience, The Tiger,* a poem of the second type.

The apparent simplicity of *The Lamb* is best considered in the light of the complexity of *The Tiger,* which will therefore be considered first. Even *The Tiger,* however, will yield considerable enjoyment to the reader through a direct approach, without the assistance of outside information, although further approaches will give additional understanding and pleasure.

The direct approach - rhythm and imagery

The direct approach depends very much on the reader's personal response to the surface meaning of the poem and the way in which that meaning is enhanced by those qualities that have an immediate impact, such as rhythm and imagery.

Activity

Re-read *The Tiger* (p. 34). What are the qualities of the poem that immediately strike you?

Discussion

Both the rhythm and imagery of *The Tiger* are likely to have made an impact on you. The rhythm seizes attention immediately with the exciting and emphatic stress on the first of each pair of syllables (*TIger! TIger! BURNing BRIGHT*). Similarly the repetition of *What* sounds through the earlier part of the poem like a series of hammer blows, coming to a climax in the fourth verse. Apart from the rhythm the visual appeal is strong. The image of the tiger stands out in bright contrast to the *forests of the night*. The sparkling of the *stars* perhaps links them with *spears* and then *tears* (17-18), which can also sparkle in the light. At the same time there is perhaps a progression in these images from something cold and aggressive to something more human and soft. Rhythm and imagery give the poem a structure, while combining to convey the poet's awe and wonder at the fierce beauty of the tiger, and at the same time lending urgency to his questions about the nature of its creator, suggested not only in the line *Did he who made the lamb make thee?*, but also in the subtle shift from *Could* in 4 to *Dare* in 24.

You may feel that a response to the poem on this level is an adequate one, or indeed the only satisfactory one possible, but nevertheless it does leave a number of questions unanswered that many readers would like answered.

Activity

List any questions that remain about the meaning of the poem.

Discussion

Questions about the overall meaning might well include:

Are we to admire or to fear the tiger?

What does it represent?

Did *he who made the lamb* make the tiger?

If so what sort of creator is he?

Questions about the details of the poem might include:
What are we to understand by *the forests of the night?*
And by *distant deeps or skies?*
How can stars throw spears and when did they?

Now, if you felt that the direct approach was the only valid way to appreciate the poem, you might well argue that to put questions in this way is to take the poem in a perversely literal manner and that the text must simply stand as it is and be accepted for what it is without further analysis. Such an approach, however, would be very limiting, and so we shall go on to consider a number of additional and complementary approaches as well, in the hope that the examination of one poem will give you a pointer as to how you might better appreciate the rest of them.

Approach through context

Up to this point we have looked at *The Tiger* in total isolation, but it is, of course, part of a larger whole. Blake completed the *Songs of Innocence* in 1789 and the *Songs of Experience* by 1794, but he always sold the latter bound together with the former. If, therefore, we wish to try to answer the question *Did he who made the lamb make thee?*, it is entirely reasonable at this point to relate *The Tiger* to its context within the *Songs* as a whole and to take up the reference to the *lamb* and look back to the poem of that name in the earlier book.

Activity

Read *The Lamb* (p. 7). Is this just a poem about an animal, or is a deeper significance attached to the lamb? What similarities and what contrasts are there between *The Lamb* and *The Tiger?*

Discussion

It is clear that the lamb is not simply the animal, nor yet simply an example of a meek and innocent creature, for it is linked with Jesus as Lamb of God and as creator (the child tells the lamb that its maker is *called by thy name*). It can now be seen that the question in *The Tiger*, *Did he who made the lamb make thee?*, may not simply be pointing to two extremes of creation, but may be setting the concept of a ruthless creator god against that of a self-sacrificing, loving god. (The title Lamb of God reminds us that Jesus was sacrificed on the cross to make possible an escape from sin, just as the Passover lamb was sacrificed by the Jews to make possible an escape from Egypt: the Jews marked their door-posts with the blood of the sacrificed lambs so that the Angel of Death passed over their houses while killing the firstborn of the Egyptians, thus persuading Pharaoh to let the Jews go.) To decide whether it is reasonable to see such a contrast in the poem between the cruel creator of the Tiger and the loving Lamb of God is difficult. If you wish to try to reach a conclusion, or at any rate to be in a position to consider the alternative arguments, then you will need to move beyond a direct response to the poem, or even to the collection of poems as a whole, and look elsewhere for further help.

Some knowledge of Blake's life and ideas will provide a framework of reference which will make it easier to respond to his poetry and to the questions (like the one above) that it poses. This does not mean that it will then become possible to know all the 'right answers', but it does mean that you are more likely to respond in an appropriate way. Care is needed here: Blake himself would have been very disapproving of the impossible attempt to pin down the 'meaning' of his poems in a paraphrase. Writing of some of his designs for illustrating a book he said: *That which can be made explicit to the idiot is not worth my care.* (Letter to the Revd Dr Trusler, 23 August 1799.) His appeal is to the imaginative insight rather than to the cold intellect.

Approach through Blake's beliefs and thought
Myth
Blake's beliefs are not easily summarized, but some of them are powerfully expressed in *The Marriage of Heaven and Hell* which was etched about 1793 (four years after *Innocence* and when most of the poems in *Experience* had been written). Conven-

tional moral values of the time are challenged. *Good, he says, is the passive that obeys Reason. Evil is the active springing from Energy.* He goes on to praise this creative energy, saying that it is *Eternal Delight.*

In other poems written at this time he establishes a mythology in which there is a restrictive, law-giving figure called Urizen, in some ways like Jehova in the Old Testament as Blake saw him, but also representing a limiting concern with the material world that leaves no room for the spirit or the imagination. Against him is set the flaming figure of Orc who represents energy and rebellion in the cause of liberty. With this knowledge that Blake's hero is a figure of fire it is possible to see that he may well feel approval for the energy of the tiger *burning bright* rather than see it as something evil. Indeed, if its burning energy is associated with that of Orc, then it may well share its creator with the *lamb* that symbolizes another approach to setting man free.

Blake saw both religious and social laws as being unjust, frustrating and perverting energy and desire (*Prisons are built with stones of law, brothels with bricks of religion – The Marriage of Heaven and Hell*). Such laws condemned natural and good instincts, while permitting, even encouraging, such wickedness as the inhumanity inflicted on innocent children as typified in the chimney-sweeper and the little black slave-boy. Given Blake's indignation at such injustice, is it possible to see the hand that *dare seize the fire* to create the energy of the tiger as being like that of another rebel who protected man's interests against an unjust god? One of the classical legends tells how Prometheus stole fire from the gods for the sake of man and also, according to the Roman poet Ovid (whom Blake had read), created man with the approval of the goddess Athene. Prometheus, then, is both a creator and one who *dared seize the fire* for the sake of mankind, and he is often presented in literature as the just rebel who fought and suffered for freedom (he was nailed to a rock for thirty thousand years by Zeus, the king of the gods). This is not to say that Blake is referring directly to Prometheus in his poem, but knowledge of the legend does give an extra insight into the poem's possible meaning.

An alternative approach is to turn to Blake's reading of mystical and neo-Platonic writers (See pp. 108-9) and to examine the imagery from these sources that Blake also uses. One critic who takes this approach (Kathleen Raine[1]) comes to the conclusion that the *forests of the night* represent creation and the evil in it. She also has a slightly different explanation of the stars throwing down their spears, associating them with the overthrow of a rebellious demi-god capable of creation, not unlike Blake's un-Biblical Satan or Messiah in *The Marriage of Heaven and Hell* who *fell, and formed a heaven of what he stole from the abyss*. Ultimately, too, this approach leads to the answer that he who made the lamb *did* make the tiger as well, for contraries do, in fact, work together; to quote again from *The Marriage of Heaven and Hell: Without contraries is no progression. Attraction and repulsion, reason and energy, love and hate, are necessary to human existence.* (For a further discussion of this see pp. 123-6.)

Religion

Another way of assessing Blake's beliefs is to see how he reacted to the religious writings of his century, particularly hymns. Is he consciously adapting the vigorously joyful rhythm of Wesley's great Christmas and Easter hymns (*Hark how all the welkin rings* · later adapted as *Hark the herald angels sing* · and *Love's redeeming work is done*) to express his own equally vigorous vision, while emphasizing just how disturbing his alternative vision is by means of the contrast? Or when he talks of stars throwing down their spears did he have in mind Isaac Watts's triumphal vision of a rather militaristic-seeming god:

> Lord of the armies of the sky
> He marshals all the stars.
> Red comets lift their banners high
> And wide proclaim his wars.

---

1. Kathleen Raine, *Blake and Antiquity* (London) 1979, pp.76-7.

If so, are we to assume that Blake's poem describes the overthrow of such a god, or that even the followers of the creator of the tiger are appalled by what he has created?

One of the most interesting comparisons of all is that with a verse translation of the Latin hymn *Dies Irae*, 'The Day of Judgment', written a century earlier by Richard Crashaw (1613-1649). Here again is a possible source for the rhythm, and also for some of the imagery, of *The Tiger*. The poet describes the fire of Judgment Day and links it with the angry, burning light of the judge's eyes which will provide the only light in the night of the end of the world, just as Blake's tiger burns *bright In the forests of the night*:

> O that fire! before whose face
> Heaven and earth shall find no place.
> O those eyes! whose angry light
> Must be the day of that dread Night.

Like Blake, Crashaw also describes the horror of the stars:

> Ah then, poor soul, what wilt thou say?
> And to what Patron choose to pray?
> When stars themselves shall stagger; and
> The most firm foot no more then stand.

Here are images which suggest that Blake might well have had judgment in mind when he wrote *The Tiger*. Furthermore Crashaw's translation introduces the idea of the weak lamb, but here as the sinner who hopes to be saved despite the terror of the Day of Judgment, since he was the *cause* that God became man in Jesus and *lost* his life on the cross to redeem him:

> Dear, remember in that Day
> Who was the cause thou cam'st this way.
> Thy sheep was strayed; And thou would'st be
> Even lost thyself in seeking me.

Activity

Does Crashaw's poem help you to answer the question *Did he who made the lamb make thee?*

Discussion

In Crashaw's poem, at any rate, the creator of the tiger-like violence of judgment can also show pity for the lamb that he has created. Perhaps in Blake's poem also it is possible that *he who made the lamb made thee* and that the violence of the tiger's 'judgment' is not wholly destructive. Nevertheless these verbal echoes are obviously not enough to 'prove' anything about Blake's meaning. All they can do is to suggest some of the ideas against which Blake may have reacted to produce his own unique response.

Politics

One of the most likely sources of imagery for *The Tiger* can be found in contemporary political writing. Once again, as in the case of Blake's response to religious writings, it is possible to see how he reacted to the ideas of others. One political pamphlet of the period, attacking the French Revolution, describes the revolutionaries as a *tigerish multitude* and observes that the *wanton cruelty of the tiger is to be claimed exclusively by the democracy.* William Wordsworth, who supported the earlier stages of the Revolution, said of Paris in 1792 that it was:

... at the best a place of fear
Unfit for the repose which night requires,
Defenceless as a wood where tigers roam.

(1805 Prelude 10, 80-2)

Wordsworth was writing after the events, but it seems clear that he was using imagery that was current at the period when Blake was writing *The Tiger*, because in 1792 Samuel Romilly wrote as follows about the founding of a French republic: *One might as well think of establishing a republic of tigers in some forest of Africa.*

Activity

This association of the revolutionaries with tigers offers an obvious interpretation of the poem, but what difference is there in the way in which Blake uses the image?

Discussion

The other writers clearly use the tiger image to suggest the savagery of the revolution, but Blake, while using the image to suggest fierce power, also seems very conscious of its *burning* beauty and *symmetry*, as one would expect of a supporter of the revolution.[2]

But does this answer all our questions? Is it enough now to say that the *forests of the night* are simply the violent streets of revolutionary Paris? Such a neat solution would appear to ignore the open-ended nature of Blake's evocative imagery. You need to bear in mind all the references mentioned above, but at the same time it is vital that you should not lose hold of your original response to the direct power and appeal of the poem's imagery.

Blake's vision

In much of what has been written so far you may feel that too much meaning is being attributed to what is quite simple and straightforward. It is appropriate, therefore, at this stage to consider what Blake had to say about the quality he called vision. He distinguished between various degrees of imaginative insight and a narrowly literal vision of the senses which he associated with the inhibiting and restrictive use of reason. He called this limited vision *single vision*, associating it with Newton's explanation, based on reason and supported by observation, of how the law of gravity makes the planets of the solar system revolve around the sun. Such a view of the universe missed all that Blake felt to be important, as he made clear some years later when he was to write:

2. See Stewart Crehan, *Blake in Context* (Dublin) 1984.

> 'What,' it will be questioned, 'when the sun rises, do you
> not see a round disk of fire somewhat like a guinea?' Oh
> no, no! I see an innumerable company of the heavenly
> host crying 'Holy, holy, holy is the Lord God Almighty!'
>
> *(Vision of the Last Judgement)*

Twofold vision he associated with creative energy and the ability to see deeper meanings beneath the physical appearance of things. He gives an example of this in his verse letter to Thomas Butts of 1802 when he describes how he had seen a thistle with his *outward* eye, but that it had been *an old man grey* to his *inward eye*:

> What to others a trifle appears
> Fills me full of smiles or tears.
> For double the vision my eyes do see,
> And a double vision is always with me.
>
> (25-28)

The threefold vision Blake refers to in the quotation below as *soft Beulah's night*. Beulah was the land reached by Christian in John Bunyan's *The Pilgrim's Progress* (1678) at the end of the journey of life as he prepared to pass from this world to the next; it was a place where the *Shining Ones commonly walked*. Consequently for Blake it is a place of visions between this material world and the world of the spirit. The final fourfold vision has a fullness which may only be caught very rarely in moments of supreme inspiration when the material world falls away to leave spiritual reality completely unveiled. Blake describes these different levels of vision in his verse letter to Thomas Butts as follows:

> Now I a fourfold vision see,
> And a fourfold vision is given to me.
> 'Tis fourfold in my supreme delight
> And threefold in soft Beulah's night
> And twofold always. May God us keep
> From single vision and Newton's sleep!
>
> (83-88)

It is Blake's habit of seeing things with the eye of imagination that justifies our concern to see beyond outward appearances in his poetry. Nevertheless there still remain some more down-to-earth approaches to be considered.

Approach through Blake's method of drafting his poems

Blake was much attached to his younger brother, Robert, and nursed him through his final illness in 1786. He told how at his death he saw his brother's spirit ascending to heaven *clapping his hands for joy* (another example of Blake's vision). He clearly regarded Robert as a kindred spirit and a source of inspiration, and he took over his partially used notebook for a number of sketches and for the drafts of many of the poems in *Songs*. *The Tiger* appears in this notebook in three main versions. In the first the horror of the tiger is strongly stressed in such phrases as *horrid ribs* and *eyes of fury*. The second version is much milder, consisting basically of verses 1, 3, 5 and 6 of the final version, although the word *Dare* is used in both first and last verses. The critic Martin Nurmi[3] suggests that the writing of the first version may have coincided with the sense of disillusion and horror amongst liberal English supporters of the French Revolution during the Terror when they felt that their ideals were being betrayed by the violence of the extreme revolutionaries, and the second more optimistic version with the end of the Terror. He also suggests a different explanation for the image of the stars throwing down their spears which first appears in the second version: he sees the creator of the tiger smiling (Blake even considered the word *laugh*, but crossed it out) *because* its creation has led to the overthrow of the forces of kingly tyranny in France, represented by the stars which throw down their spears in surrender. (One of his reasons for suggesting this is that in Blake's *The French Revolution* the king's armies

---

3. Martin K. Nurmi, Blake's Revisions of 'The Tyger' in *Songs of Innocence and Experience, A Casebook,* ed. Margaret Bottrall (London) 1970, pp. 198-217.

are described as *starry hosts*). This alternative explanation is a useful reminder that there is often more than one side to an argument, but in fact Nurmi goes on to argue that in its final form the poem moves away from the particular events of 1792-3 and that in restoring something of the tiger's dreadfulness in the final version Blake achieves a balance between the contrary aspects of the tiger, creating a powerful symbol of similar significance to that which Kathleen Raine proposes.

Blake's printing methods

There remains one important piece of evidence when interpreting Blake's poems and that is the way in which they were first printed. Blake did not receive a formal academic education, but went first to a drawing school and then on to an apprenticeship with the engraver Basire. After this he studied at the Royal Academy of Art. He was thus a trained artist, and an integral part of his conception of many of his poems was the designs which surrounded them. He tells how Robert appeared to him in a dream after his death and explained to him how to etch both text and design on the same plate and print them together. The pages produced in this way were then coloured by hand and bound together, but not always in the same order. There are twenty-one copies of *Songs of Innocence* and a further twenty-seven of *Songs of Innocence and of Experience* combined, but no separate copies of *Songs of Experience*, which Blake obviously considered to be an integral part of the expanded work.

Blake's experiments with the order do not seem to be random and certainly serve to illustrate various ways in which the poems can throw light on each other. In the order followed in this edition the fierce energy of *The Tiger* stands out in strong contrast to the petty fears that lead to the false modesty of *The Angel* and the jealousy of *My Pretty Rose Tree*.

For some of the songs the pictures and decorations appear to be no more than literally illustrative, but some are highly suggestive both in symbolic detail and in evoking mood.

Activity

Look at the illustration for *The Tiger* on p. 144. How effectively does it match or add to the mood and meaning of the poem?

Discussion

At first sight it has to be admitted that the picture of the tiger is rather disappointing. One critic suggests two reasons for this: firstly that a totally realistic tiger would encourage the reader to think in literal terms instead of considering the energy it represents, and secondly that Blake has tried to incorporate human features into the tiger's face to show that the same qualities can be found in man [4]. Some would argue, however, that this particular illustration quite simply fails to match the accompanying text in the intensity of its artistic vision.

The next section will consider some aspects of Blake's imagery and style and a final section on p. 111 will consider Blake's times and thought, with reference to the *Songs* as a whole.

Imagery

Much imagery has a direct appeal which might be expected to provoke a similar response from nearly all readers, but this is not always the case.

Activity

Consider the following list taken from the *Songs* and divide them into those with pleasant and those with unpleasant associations: children at play, the lamb, thorns, a cage, flowers of London town (describing the charity children gathered at their annual service at St Paul's), an iron chain, swaddling bands, briars, manacles, a dimpling stream.

Discussion

Most people will probably divide those into two groups, the 'pleasant' group relating to the innocence and attractiveness of childhood and the 'unpleasant' relating to restriction and pain:

---

4. John Beer, *Blake's Humanism* (Manchester) 1968, p. 67.

children at play	thorns
lamb	cage
flowers of London town	iron chain
dimpling stream	briars
	manacles

But which category should *swaddling bands* come into? It is now an old-fashioned word and may well remind you of the traditional telling of the story of Christ's birth. Do you put it therefore in the first category? On the other hand these children's clothes are *bands* bound tightly and restrictively around the child. Should they therefore be in the second category? It is only when you examine the context and discover that the resentful child is *striving against* the *swaddling bands* that you can reach a conclusion. (See *Infant Sorrow* p. 40.)

Fresh interpretations of familiar images

The importance of the context of an image becomes clearer if you consider now the *humble sheep*. This might well be associated with the innocent lamb, but this would be a mistake.

Activity

Read *The Lily* (p. 36) and consider what the difference is between the rose and the sheep on the one hand and the lily on the other.

Discussion

It would appear that the kind of innocence that the *sheep* achieves by fending off *love* with its *horn* and refusing to *delight* in it is not true innocence at all. The white *lily*, however, does represent purity as you might expect, but it turns out that this purity does not depend on sexual abstinence, for it can *in love delight*. In other words Blake's challenging of the conventional values of the time is accompanied by a refusal to accept the conventional associations of familiar images. The conventional idea (white lily = purity) is recognized, but only as the starting point for a new approach which sees no conflict between innocence and love.

Where Blake does use an image in a traditional way it is still with a lively awareness of how it can be given fresh meaning. The image of the rose has long been associated with the beauty of woman and when Blake's near contemporary, Robert Burns, uses it, it does indeed seem well-worn, merely letting us know that the man finds the woman attractive:

O, my Luve's like a red red rose
That's newly sprung in June.

Activity

Look at the illustration of *The Sick Rose* (p. 142) and read the text of *My Pretty Rose Tree* (p. 35) and *The Lily* (p. 36). What is the inevitable accompaniment of the rose for Blake that is missing from Burns's poem?

Discussion

The thorns serve as a reminder that love and beauty are not always accessible; in *My Pretty Rose Tree*, for example, they represent an unreasonable jealousy that keeps the man at bay. Elsewhere they are used to represent the restrictions of a repressive moral code *binding with briars my joys and desires* (*The Garden of Love*, p. 36).

Meaningful ambiguity

Just as the thorns are one sign that Blake's use of rose imagery is far from the easy sentimentality of Burns, so too is the use of another traditional image in *The Sick Rose*, that of the worm. Here, however, the interpretation of the image is very much open to debate. Literally it is the maggot that bores its way through the rose and prevents it coming to full bloom, but there are many other associations.

Activity

How many of the following seem relevant?

a) The worm of conscience or passion that secretly troubles a person, as when Shakespeare makes Queen Margaret say to the future Richard III: *The worm of conscience still begnaw thy soul!* (*Richard III* 1, 3);

b) Satan, called *that false worm* by Milton (*worm* can mean serpent), who entered Paradise to corrupt Eve who was the *fairest flower* (*Paradise Lost 9*, 1068, 432);

c) the earthworm that supposedly eats corpses (in some of the illustrations the worm is banded like an earthworm);

d) a phallic symbol hinting at the destructiveness of sexual passion.

Discussion

You may find some of these suggestions unhelpful, but you may also find that some of them are by no means mutually exclusive and that, when taken together, they provide an enriched meaning. The same approach is fruitful in reading many of the other poems as well.

Activity

Just such an ambiguity exists in the opening of *London*:

I wander through each chartered street,

Near where the chartered Thames does flow.

Is *chartered* to be interpreted as free or the very opposite? Read the note on p. 78-9 and consider whether the conflicting explanations can be seen as two sides of the same coin.

Discussion

You may well feel confident that you know which of the possible meanings was Blake's primary one, but nevertheless in choosing the word he has also, it seems, chosen to remind us of the alternative view: that of the citizen proud of his city's charter, or perhaps pleased to have purchased land or to have entered into a profitable contract; such transactions have increased the citizen's material freedom, but are arguably based on a loss of freedom for the less privileged. We are left with a table in which the meanings of charter might look rather like this:

Privilege =	Exclusion
Royal Grant =	Submission of Subjects
Conveyancing =	Selling Property that should be Common to All
Hiring =	Making Goods Available only to those with Wealth

That Blake was forcing a re-evaluation of a popular concept seems clear from a comparison with the contrasting use of *charter* in *Rule Britannia*, written in 1740 and popular ever since: *This was the charter ... Britons never ... shall be slaves.*

Biblical imagery

It should now be clear that even the most directly appealing of Blake's images need to be carefully considered. The initial impact is important, but often there is more to be discovered than lies on the surface. One area where many of us are at a disadvantage to Blake's original readers is in grasping the full implications of his Biblical imagery, since Blake would have taken for granted a depth of knowledge which is rare nowadays. Biblical quotations have been given where appropriate in the notes to individual poems, but if you look them up and read them in their biblical context they will begin to mean much more to you. In any case no single reference can ever give you the full range of associations of an image such as that of the *marks* in *London*. For one thing there are ambiguities very similar to those of chartered which can only be tackled by considering the possible source texts.

Activity

First re-read the opening stanza of *London* given below and then consider the meaning of *mark* and *marks*:

> I wander through each chartered street,
> Near where the chartered Thames does flow,
> And mark in every face I meet
> Marks of weakness, marks of woe.

Discussion

Presumably the basic meaning of *mark* in 3 is 'notice', although it might mean 'make a mark', as in the example from *Romans* given in paragraph *a*). In 4, *marks* may be taken to mean 'signs'. These meanings give satisfactory sense, but an awareness of some of the biblical uses of *mark* opens up a fascinating range of supplementary readings which force the reader to consider what Blake's attitude is to the citizens of London and thereby enrich the poem.

a) After Cain had murdered his brother Abel *the Lord set a mark upon* [him], *lest any finding him should kill him* (*Genesis 4,15*). Furthermore St Paul tells the Romans in his epistle to *mark them which cause divisions and offences ... and avoid them* (*Romans 16, 17*). Are we to assume therefore that the passers-by in the streets of London are guilty outcasts like Cain and disturbers of the peace who are being *marked* so that they can be avoided? Do the ideas of *weakness* and *woe* tie in with this?

b) A much more sympathetic reference would be to *Ezekiel 9*, in which God commands: *Go through the midst of the city, through the midst of Jerusalem, and set a mark upon the foreheads of the men that sigh and that cry for all the abominations that be done in the midst thereof*. God then commands that the wicked should be slain, *but come not near any man upon whom is the mark*. In this case may we assume that the marks indicate pity, a willingness to show mercy to the downtrodden who bear the *marks of weakness, marks of woe*?

c) A third possibility remains if we turn to *Revelation 13, 17*, where there is a reference to the *beast*, which in Blake's terms could well be the power of the Church and State, and where we are told that those who carry the mark of the beast are forced to do so if they are to engage in the normal business of life: *no man might buy or sell, save he that had the mark ... of the beast.* Here perhaps is a symbol of the subservience of the masses to the *beast*, which might provoke our pity. When we read the next chapter, however, we discover that no pity is offered, for an angel announces: *If any man worship the beast and his image, and receive his mark in his forehead, or in his hand, the same shall drink of the wine of the wrath of God (Revelation 14, 9-10).* Is the *mark* a sign of guilt after all and of the inevitability of punishment?[5]

Such a variety of reference may seem to create more problems than it solves, but does offer the possibility of a much richer appreciation of the poem than might at first have been apparent. As with the use of the word *chartered* the question arises as to whether the interpretations have to be mutually exclusive or whether they can not only co-exist, but also throw useful light on each other.

Imagery derived from myth

The imagery that Blake derives from myth is less important in the *Songs* than elsewhere in his poetry, but there is one important myth which is arguably the source of a number of images in the *Songs*. There was a neo-Platonist theory (derived from the belief of the Greek philosopher Plato in the immortality of the soul) that the soul existed before birth. When the soul entered the body at birth it was, as it were, entering a prison and suffering a loss of freedom that was paradoxically closer to death than life. Thus the physical body can even perhaps be thought of as a coffin from which the soul is set free at death to return to full freedom and life (*The Chimney-Sweeper* [*Innocence*] 14 - p. 20). Physical existence is seen in this mythology as moisture, as in the clouds that are the bodies of the two children in *The Little Black Boy* 23 (p. 14) and the infant in *Infant Sorrow* 4 (p. 40), or as in the *wat'ry shore* on which Earth is imprisoned in *Earth's Answer* 6 (p. 28), or the water of the

---

5. I am indebted for the ideas in this section to Edward Larrissy, *William Blake*, (Oxford) 1985.

brook in *The Clod and the Pebble* (p. 29). Nevertheless if *The Little Girl Lost* and *The Little Girl Found* (p. 3) are to be interpreted as a version of this myth of the descent of the soul into physical life, then the experience is not necessarily unpleasant.

Activity

In the light of the above consider whether the grave in *Ah! Sunflower* (p. 35) and the cage in *The Schoolboy* (p.12) can be images of the body.

Discussion

If the *sweet golden clime Where the traveller's journey is done* is not merely that place in the heavens where the sun goes at the end of the day, but also the heaven that is reached after the *journey* of life is *done*, then it is not unreasonable to see the youth and the virgin as wishing to leave the *graves* of their bodies to reach the *sweet golden clime* of heaven. In *The Schoolboy* the cage seems most obviously to be an image of the school in which the boy is trapped, but a secondary interpretation could be that the bird is the soul trapped in the body, just as the boy's soul is trapped in both the body and the uncongenial upbringing that his parents have imposed on him.

Activity

Is the view of physical life offered in *To Tirzah* similar?

Discussion

The apparent contradiction implied in the oxymoron of *mortal birth* (*mortal* contrasts with *birth* since it means *subject to death* as well as *human*) certainly seems to support the view of human life being a kind of death for the soul. Notice how the idea is emphasized further when Blake writes of being *betrayed* to *mortal life*.

Repeated images

One important aspect of the imagery in the *Songs* is the way in which Blake uses it to develop certain ideas from one poem to another. The rose with its accompanying thorns is one image which has already been mentioned as serving such a purpose.

Sometimes these echoes help to create a similar atmosphere, while at other times they serve to strengthen a point by contrast. Both approaches can be seen in the treatment of the village green which is a place for innocent play in both *The Echoing Green* and the first *Nurse's Song*, but is then a place for jealous repression in the second *Nurse's Song*, and finally a place *filled with graves, And tomb-stones where flowers should be* in *The Garden of Love*. The power of the image in this last poem derives at least in part from the fact that we have already seen the green in a context of innocent and unrestricted love, and thus have a vivid sense of what was lost when *A chapel was built in the midst*.

Activity

Explore for yourself how this image of the *Chapel* is itself reinforced by other references to priest, church and altar in *The Chimney-Sweeper (Experience)*, *The Little Vagabond* and *A Little Boy Lost*.

Discussion

The cluster of images relating to the church paints a picture of an organization that consistently exploits, represses and punishes the young and the poor and outcast, but offers nothing in exchange.

The overall impression is damning indeed and it is not restricted to the priests, for in *A Little Girl Lost* we see the father behaving very similarly to the priest of *A Little Boy Lost*. It is true that the father appears different at first sight, for he gives his daughter a *loving look*, but this is compared to the *holy book* and has the effect of terrifying her, and although he trembles with *fear* rather than *zeal*, he shares with the priest the desire to restrict natural emotion.

There are other images which would re-pay examination in this way: for example consider what is surprising about the lion's tears in *Night* and *The Little Girl Lost* and what the two situations have in common that explains the surprising image. Again in the same two poems and in *A Cradle Song* compare the atmosphere that the references to the moon help to create, or consider in what way the repeated image of the poison tree in the poem of that name and *The Human Abstract* enables the two poems to throw light upon each other.

Activity

What themes from *Songs* are brought together in *London*? What is the effect of gathering them together in this way?

Discussion

Children at play or suffering, chimney-sweeps, slave-boys, boys and girls controlled by parents, priests, schoolmasters, nurses, all are found throughout the *Songs*, and so when we hear of *every infant's cry of fear* all the suffering of the children described elsewhere is summed up; we already know the bitterly appropriate pun of the chimney-sweeper's cry: *weep, weep*, just as we know the *church* is black with more than soot and is indeed actively *black'ning*, as *the priests in black gowns* destroy the possibility of happiness, *binding with briars my joys and desires*. Furthermore, this restriction of love, bound not only by the *briars* of the priest but by the *trembling fear* of such as Ona's father, has led to its perversion and corruption; hence the *youthful harlot's curse* which affects the would-be lovers not only with the literal plague of venereal disease, but also with the plagues of the lovelessness and frustration of the *green and pale* nurse or of the speaker in *The Angel*, with the plague of the secret corruption of *The Sick Rose*, and with the plague of the jealousy of *My Pretty Rose Tree*.

Blake's times

Revolutions

Despite the unique quality of Blake's vision, his preoccupations are very much with the world in which he lived, and some knowledge of this is necessary if an adequate approach is to be made to his poetry. His lifetime covers a period in which the groundwork was beginning to be laid for two of the things which we take for granted in the western world: democracy and material wealth on a previously unimagined scale. Neverthe-less, the political revolutions elsewhere (see p. 89), which gave voice to the ideals of freedom, led only to repression in Britain, while the Industrial Revolution at first led only to wealth for the few and actually worsened conditions for the poor.

Rousseau

It may seem strange to start this survey of revolutionary times with the work of a Swiss writer whose name was scorned by Blake on account of his free-thinking rejection of religion. Nevertheless, Jean-Jacques Rousseau (1712-1778) had a pow-erful and truly revolutionary influence on the way in which people thought in the latter part of the eighteenth century and many of his ideas are found in Blake's work. He saw the society in which he lived as separating man from nature and thus causing the loss of happiness and virtue. The constraints society imposed on people forced them to conform and to disguise their true feelings, and this alienated them from their fellows. This loss of self-sufficiency led to a competitive striving for superiority and to the evils of greed and property.

Rousseau saw the solution to these problems in a recognition of the rights of the under-privileged and of the importance of natural feeling. In a just society there would be a *social contract* and the law would reflect the *general will* of the people. This idealistic belief that the *general will* would be an expression of the conscience of the people, which all would freely obey, was based on the assumption that within every person there was an *innate principle of justice and virtue* and that a new approach to education could preserve this. The child's natural instincts would be honoured and he would learn through experiences which stimulated his intelligence. Ideas would not be imposed on him in a dictatorial manner by adults, but learnt by the child for himself.

Blake has little to say directly about the concept of a *social contract*, although he makes the need for it clear in *The Human Abstract*, where in the absence of a *general will* for good it is only *mutual fear* that *brings Peace*, and that only *Till the selfish loves increase* (p. 39). The needs, however, that prompt Rousseau to put forward his concept of the *social contract*, the need for justice for the under-privileged and the need for natural feelings to flourish rather than be warped by society, are very much at the heart of the *Songs*.

Activity

Many of the *Songs* show the warping of the natural instincts of innocence. Consider what the consequences of this warping are, as described in *The Human Abstract* (p. 39).

Discussion

Even virtues are seen as being no more than the consequences of an unjust society. *Pity* and *Mercy*, after all, should not be necessary *If all were as happy as we*, while Humility is either hypocritical or, if sincere, reflects a loss of wholesome self-respect which is replaced instead with *selfish loves*. This selfishness is seen to provoke greed, fear, cruelty, the false religion of *Mystery*, and deceit. All this comes from the perversion of what, Blake as well as Rousseau feel, should be naturally good if only not warped, namely the *human brain*.

Revolution in America

Blake came to manhood at the time of the American Revolution, which was prompted by the American colonists' objections to being taxed by the British Parliament in which they were not represented; it was the first successful attempt in modern times to establish democracy and the freedom and rights of the individual. In 1776 the American Declaration of Independence had made the same claim as Rousseau that governments derived their authority not from inherited privilege, but from the will of the people:

> We hold these truths to be self-evident, that all men are created equal, that they are endowed by their Creator with certain inalienable Rights, that among these are Life, Liberty and the pursuit of Happiness – That to secure these rights, Governments are instituted among Men, deriving their just powers from the consent of the governed.

Tom Paine was a radical English writer who supported both the American and the French revolutions with his pamphlets. Paine, who was later to become acquainted with Blake and with whose ideas Blake sympathized, had this to say in the year of the American Declaration of Independence:

> Government, like dress, is the badge of lost innocence; the palaces of kings are built upon the ruins of the bowers of paradise.

Activity

Blake does not write directly about political matters in the *Songs*, but consider how authority (if not literally *Government*) crushes *the bowers of paradise* and prevents the *pursuit of Happiness* by imposing restrictions on the innocent freedom of the young in *The Schoolboy* (p. 12) and *The Garden of Love* (p. 36).

Discussion

As you might expect, the innocence of youth is shown as warped or restricted by adult control in many of the poems in *Experience*, but some of the poems that were intended to portray *the bowers of paradise* in *Innocence* also show how it can be crushed. A particularly clear picture of the *paradise* that is lost by adult intervention is given in *The Schoolboy,* which was originally in *Innocence*, but later transferred to *Experience*; it describes the bird-song on a *summer morn* that can no longer be appreciated once the boy is at school under the *cruel eye outworn* of his schoolmaster. *The Garden of Love* in *Experience* takes up Paine's image even more closely with its account of the repressive chapel built *Where I used to play on the green* and its illustration of two young people kneeling under the direction of a priest in black.

A 'Revolution' at home

Nevertheless it would be a mistake to assume that Blake's view of life in his earlier poems is entirely pessimistic. It is clear that in the 1780s in Blake's own parish of St James's, Piccadilly, attempts were being made to improve the lot of the poor. Many babies had been dying in the workhouse and a new policy was started of sending them out to foster-mothers in Wimbledon, which at that time was outside London. This resulted in a quite remarkable improvement in the survival rate. The pictures of adults at one with the children in their charge in *The Echoing Green* and the first *Nurse's Song* may well reflect a hopefulness based on this exceptional humanitarian endeavour.[6]

Activity

Read *Spring* and *Infant Joy*. In what ways do these poems express an optimistic delight in childhood?

Discussion

Blake's almost 'feminine' sympathy with the simple delight of mothers or nurses in young children can be seen in the emotional rather than reasoned approach of *Spring* (compare *The Blossom* and *Laughing Song*). This approach is reflected in the looseness of the grammatical form, which avoids structured and restricting statements and is content to be impressionistic. A 'feminine' acceptance of life's simple joys can perhaps be seen in *Infant Joy* as well, but this poem has an insistently repetitive structure. This could be seen as a way of emphasizing the bliss of the mother who is happy simply to sing over her baby's cradle, but it might on the other hand be seen as a way of putting words into the infant's mouth in what would then be a rather restrictive manner.

The survival of so many children who would previously have died then raised the problem of how to educate them subseqently. A new parish school of industry was established where the children could board, instead of being sent back to the over-crowded and unhealthy workhouse. In its early years, furthermore, it seems that a real, and exceptional, attempt was made to provide good education, although later it deteriorated.

6 The information here is derived from Stanley Gardner, *Blake's Innocence and Experience Retraced*, (London) 1986.

Whatever Blake may say in *The Schoolboy* about schoolmasters, there was something almost revolutionary in educating the poor 'above their station' in this way which may have met with his approval.

Activity

Read *The Shepherd*. Could this be seen in some way as a 'contrary' poem to *The Schoolboy*, expressing approval of the way in which children were being brought up?

Discussion

If the caring relationship between shepherd and sheep is taken to be an image of the relationship between adult and child, then the poem could be seen as expressing approval for the care offered the children of St James's parish. The care offered, however, is much more like that of the indulgent nurse of the first *Nurse's Song* than that of a schoolmaster. *The Schoolboy* is probably a better guide to Blake's feelings about the restrictive nature of formal education, however benevolent the intentions of those providing it.

Nevertheless, Blake's acceptance in some of the poems of the possibility of innocent happiness under the protection of adults means that it may be a mistake, for example, to read irony into the first *Holy Thursday* (see notes on p. 60), even if with hindsight a perhaps unintended irony emerged as Blake saw the decline of his own parish's attempt at true charity. The fact that a number of the songs in *Innocence* were subsequently placed in *Experience* is a reminder, however, that they should certainly not all be taken as delighting uncritically in the joys of innocence.

The Industrial Revolution

The other revolution that might have been expected to improve the lot of ordinary people was the Industrial Revolution. The rapid expansion of coal and iron production and the development of the steam engine paved the way for the introduction of labour-saving machinery which vastly increased industrial output, but the wealth that the Industrial Revolution created was not shared out. Indeed in Blake's lifetime the cost of living doubled, but wages rose by no more than a half. The loss of employment as manufacturing moved from cottage to factory (where women and children were more frequently employed than men and at lower wages) caused a very real poverty which was not helped by the threefold rise in the price of bread between 1790 and 1800. The crowds who moved to the towns in search of employment too often found inadequate accommodation and lived in conditions of great squalor. The disgrace of greater wealth combined with increased poverty is surely what provokes Blake's ironic exclamation in the second *Holy Thursday* which is nonetheless true for so many: *It is a land of poverty!* Furthermore the impoverishment was a spiritual one as well as a material one as Blake makes clear in *London*:

And mark in every face I meet
Marks of weakness, marks of woe.

Religious attitudes to social wrongs

In the face of these social wrongs the complacency of the church clearly seemed unforgivable to Blake. It is perhaps unfair to quote Isaac Watts's poem *Praise for Mercies Spiritual and Temporal* to illustrate this, for it was printed in 1715, long before the Industrial Revolution had made an impact on life in the towns. It is of interest all the same, not only because of the attitude to poverty it reveals, but also because it comes from Watts's *Divine Songs for the Use of Children*, which is an important example of improving poetry written for children, a model that Blake was following and perhaps, by implication, criticizing, when he wrote the earlier *Songs*:

Whene'er I take my walks abroad,
How many poor I see!
What shall I render to my God
For all his gifts to me?

Not more than others I deserve,
Yet God hath given me more;
For I have food, while others starve,
Or beg from door to door.

How many children in the street
Half-naked I behold!
While I am clothed from head to feet,
And covered from the cold.

While some poor wretches scarce can tell
Where they may lay their head,
I have a home wherein to dwell,
And rest upon my bed.

While others early learn to swear,
And curse and lie and steal,
Lord, I am taught thy name to fear,
And do thy holy will.

Are these thy favours day by day
To me above the rest?
Then let me love thee more than they,
And try to serve thee best.

Activity

Compare this poem with *The Lamb* (p. 7) and *The Shepherd* (p. 8). Do you find any differences in technique or tone?

Discussion

The simplicity of the language and the reassuring tone mean that the poems from *Innocence* have a good deal in common with the Watts poem. In *The Lamb* Blake, like Watts, uses the catechism method, i.e. the use of questions to instruct, the questions eliciting the answers that the speaker or writer wants. So there are similarities between the poems, but there is a difference of subject matter, since in his poems Blake does not touch on the miseries of the world.

Activity

Now compare the Watts poem with *The Chimney-Sweeper* (p. 20) in *Innocence*, which does tackle the issue of poverty and hardship. Both poems are supposedly spoken by children; does either poem offer an alternative, more adult, viewpoint?

Discussion

In both poems the child speaking appears to accept the cruel unfairness of life without comment, but the fact that the sweep does so is far more telling because he is a victim, whereas clearly the other child is comfortably off. Furthermore, the child in *Praise for Mercies Spiritual and Temporal* merely sees the misfortunes of others as a cause for gratitude to God without any hint that something needs to be done about the plight of the poor. The reason for this is perhaps hinted at in *The Chimney-Sweeper*, for the angel promises comfort in the next world as a consolation for the miseries of this one. Such a consolation would have have been thought a real one by most of Blake's readers, but it was hardly a justification for the callous cruelty with which sweeps were treated. If, therefore, you react with a sense of scandal to the uncomplaining voice of the sweep and the angel's lack of concern at his cruel sufferings, then you may feel that there is an extra dimension here that is lacking in the Watts poem and that Blake's irony is functioning (in other words that there is a disparity between the apparent message of the poem and its true meaning) and that the final viewpoint is Blake's own of condemnation, not the child's of acceptance.

Man's sinfulness – the doctrine of the Fall

Although many in the church were complacent about the suffering of the poor, there was an area where the church's conscience was active and that was in its insistence on man's fallen condition. The doctrine of the Fall holds that all mankind is inherently sinful and has been ever since Adam and Eve disobeyed God and ate the apple in the Garden of Eden, thus falling away from God (see *Genesis 3*). This accounting for mankind's inherent sinfulness by attributing it to *original sin*, which was thought of as being either inherited from, or shared with, Adam and Eve, was the common teaching of the church. It finds its most powerful statement in English literature in John Milton's *Paradise Lost* (1667), a poem which Blake much admired, but not for orthodox reasons. He felt that it revealed the tyranny of God towards mankind and the attractive energy of Satan; hence his famous remark that Milton was *of the Devil's party without knowing it*, (*The Marriage of Heaven and Hell* Plate 6), and hence his echoing of Milton (e.g. in *A Poison Tree*) to help express his own radical ideas.

When the doctrine of the Fall was combined with a belief, current in one section of the church, in the doctrine of pre-destination to either Heaven or Hell, it could lead to despair. The doctrine of pre-destination is that God has chosen some people from the beginning of time to be saved (the 'elect' or chosen ones) while others will inevitably be damned. Such a doctrine could understandably lead to despair, especially if you took your sinfulness as evidence that you were destined to be damned and that no effort could save you. The feelings that such beliefs provoked are well captured in the writings of another eighteenth-century poet, William Cowper (1731-1800), who referred to himself as a *destined wretch*. In his poem *Hatred and Vengeance* he speaks of himself in these terms:

Man disavows, and Deity disowns me:
Hell might afford my miseries a shelter;
Therefore hell keeps her ever-hungry mouths all
Bolted against me.

and concludes:

> I, fed with judgement, in a fleshly tomb, am
> Buried above ground.

The sense of exclusion here is frightening; Cowper even regrets the loss of shelter that hell might offer him (note how chilling is the effect of that *Therefore*). Such a sense of exclusion is only intensified by contrast with the feelings of those who are confident that they *are* among the chosen ones: Watts's child sees himself favoured *above the rest*. Blake rejects pre-destination, and it is against such despairing attitudes as Cowper's that Blake's criticisms of the teaching of the priests in *The Garden of Love* and *A Little Boy Lost* should be set.

Activity

Re-read *Earth's Answer* (p. 28). How far are the feelings of Earth comparable to the despair of the man who feels himself destined to damnation?

Discussion

One major difference is between Cowper's acceptance of his guilt and the Earth's protest that natural feelings are not evidence of original sin and that *free love* (natural desires) should not be *with bondage bound*. On the other hand you might well feel that the sense of darkness, dread and despair that Earth feels on being *Prisoned on wat'ry shore* of existence matches closely Cowper's sense of horror at being trapped in a *fleshly tomb*. The *Deity* who *disowns* Cowper is surely comparable with the *Selfish father of men*.

Rationalism in the Church

The church could also be seen to have a limited vision in its rejection of the emotional enthusiasm of Methodism and its preference for coolly reasoned arguments for the existence of God, such as that proposed by the theologian Paley; he argued that the world had clearly been constructed for a purpose and that therefore there must be a creator who had constructed it (his *Evidences of Christianity* was published in the same year that

Experience was completed). Such an argument seemed to take it for granted that man learns through his senses alone (as the philosopher Locke had claimed) and can reason his way to a recognition of God (just as Newton's understanding of the underlying principle of gravity had confirmed his belief in God as creator). Such a view, Blake felt, left no room for the visionary approach.

Blake's own ideas

Blake's own religious system is a personal one derived both from his own thoughtful response to the ideas of others and from his own particular perception of the world around him. The few poems which offer more comforting and orthodox ideas occur in *Innocence.*

Activity

Re-read *The Lamb* (p. 7) and *A Dream* (p. 2). What comfort do these poems offer in the face of life's harshness?

Discussion

Both poems were presumably written with children in mind before the scope of the *Songs* became much wider. *The Lamb* offers no hint (beyond the meaning of Lamb of God) as to the cruel nature of the death of Jesus on the cross (see notes on p. 53). We may possibly see evidence of a constrictive approach to childhood freedom in its repetitively enclosed, catechism form, but alternatively the clear structure may be seen as comforting. *A Dream* gives a picture of a world in which an all-embracing providence caters even for insects. This is perhaps even more comforting for the child, but the *experienced* reader can hardly help reflecting on the difference between this *dream* and the real world. (Another dream-like poem, *Night*, openly acknowledges that some may be *weeping* rather than *sleeping* (21-2), while the fact that *wolves and tigers howl for prey* (25), and also succeed in killing it, reminds the reader of the sorrows of this world, however beautifully the closing verses may speak of the next one.)

Swedenborg's influence

One of the most important of Blake's ideas is derived from the teaching of an unorthodox religious thinker, Emanuel Swedenborg (1688-1772). (Swedenborg himself never tried to found a separate church, but some of his followers did, and Blake attended some of the first meetings of the Swedenborgian Society in 1789, the year in which he completed *Innocence*.) Swedenborg rejected the Christian doctrine of the Trinity, which teaches the threefold nature of God as creator (God the Father), of God made human (God the Son, i.e. Jesus), and of God continuing to inspire humanity throughout time (God the Holy Spirit). Instead he argued that Jesus alone, the *Divine Human*, was God. Blake goes further, asserting that divinity is to be found within every human. He also claims that the Fall (the consequence of eating the apple in the Garden of Eden) is not the punishment for man's sinfulness by a just god, but the revenge of the *Selfish father of men* who wishes to restrict man's natural freedom.

The interlinking of human and divine is most clearly stated in the *Songs* in *The Divine Image* (p. 19), and leads to certain important conclusions for Blake about the human condition. These are implied in the *Songs* and stated more directly in *The Marriage of Heaven and Hell* which Blake wrote in between the two parts of the *Songs* and which it will be useful to quote here. Plate numbers are given for reference to all editions.

The first point is that man's instincts are not fallen (i.e. sinful from the moment of birth) and therefore to follow the instinctive desire for love and pleasure cannot be wrong: *The soul of sweet delight can never be defiled* (Plate 9, 14). On the contrary it is the thwarting of desire that leads to corruption and a warping of the personality: *Sooner murder an infant in its cradle than nurse unacted desires* (Plate 10, 8). The conventional goodness of Blake's time, therefore, is just a passive failure to act out desire and is not something positive to be admired, unlike evil which is evidence of positive energy: *Good is the passive that obeys reason. Evil is the active springing from energy* (Plate 3) and *Energy is eternal delight* (Plate 4).

If conventional morality is mistaken, it follows that those who try to enforce it are themselves immoral and have a corrupting effect: *Prisons are built with stones of law, brothels with bricks of religion* (Plate 8, 1); in other words the corruption to be found in prison or brothel has been created in the first place by the mistaken laws which have warped human behaviour. What was originally decent and attractive has been singled out for destruction: *As the caterpillar chooses the fairest leaves to lay her eggs on, so the priest lays his curse on the fairest joys* (Plate 9, 16). It follows also that it is right to denounce the corrupting influence of this false morality: *the voice of honest indignation is the voice of God* (Plates 12-13). Blake, in fact, with his insistence on the purity of natural feeling and his denunciation of the abuses of society, is closer than he might admit to Rousseau's point of view.

The other aspect of Swedenborg's thought which was congenial to Blake was his theory of correspondences, whereby material objects were only the outward and visible parts of spiritual realities. Blake, who had looked out of the window as a child and seen angels in a tree and had seen the soul of his dying brother ascend to heaven clapping his hands, had always looked beyond the surface: *If the doors of perception* [i.e. the senses] *were cleansed every thing would appear to man as it is, infinite* (Plate 14).

This affects Blake's understanding of human nature: *Man has no body distinct from his soul; for that called body is a portion of soul discerned by the five senses, the chief inlets of soul in this age* (Plate 4). In other words the outward body that we can see and feel and touch is only an outward sign of the soul, which is the true person.

False religion

Furthermore, Blake saw the alternative approach to life, which depended on sense impressions alone (as the philosopher Locke had taught) as deadening and likely to lead to the cruelty that fails to see the divine within the humanity of the little black slave or the chimney-sweep. Consequently he associated this approach, limited as it was to what could be physically observed and reasoned about, with the *Selfish father of men* that he was later to call Urizen (from the rationalist friend who used to cry *Your reason?*, or perhaps from the Greek for *to limit?*). After all, reason without vision is as limiting as a morality which over-rides natural instinct.

Activity

Consider *A Poison Tree* in the light of Blake's thoughts on human nature.

Discussion

The need to give vent to natural feelings, even if they might seem reprehensible, is made clear in *A Poison Tree* where the anger that the narrator feels towards his friend is expressed, and so ended. The anger he feels towards his foe, however, is concealed and therefore emerges in a far more destructive manner. The suppression of feeling leads not only to deceit, but also to deadly malice, and it brings out an equivalent malice and possessive greed in his foe. In this atmosphere of secretive rivalry fear proves a strong motive to evil as well.

Activity

Now consider what light *A Poison Tree* throws on Blake's view of false religion as a repressive moral code which binds *with briars my joys and desires*.

Discussion

This poem can also be seen as a re-telling of the story of the Fall, in which case the owner of the tree is a vengeful god who tempts man by forbidding him the fruit of the tree. The natural energy and curiosity of man leads him to taste the fruit and to incur death, which was unknown until the Fall. Such a picture is blasphemous by Christian standards, but it accords well with Blake's unorthodox reading of Milton's *Paradise Lost*, and with his idea of a repressive god (such as Urizen) against whom the Messiah-like figure of Orc (representing flaming energy) fights.

It relates also to the picture in *Earth's Answer* of Earth *Prisoned on wat'ry shore* by *Starry jealousy* (in other words trapped within the physical matter of this world – see p. 108 – by a jealous god). For the idea that *Starry jealousy* might be God compare: *Thou shalt have no other gods before me . . . for I the Lord thy God am a jealous God* (Ten Commandments – *Exodus, 20*).

These two readings are not mutually exclusive, for it is the repressive, death-dealing god of the second reading who provokes the human secrecy and fearful malice of the first reading.

Conclusion

Both parts of the *Songs* include poems that were written later – *The Voice of the Ancient Bard* (p. 15) was added to the end of *Innocence*, but later transferred to the end of *Experience*, and *To Tirzah* (p. 43) was added to *Experience*.

Activity

Read these poems again and consider how far they modify the final impression given by the *Songs*.

Discussion

One of the quotations from *The Marriage of Heaven and Hell* will serve as an introduction to this final point: *Without contraries is no progression. Attraction and repulsion, reason and energy, love and hate, are necessary to human existence*. The full title of the *Songs* describes them as *Showing the Two Contrary States of the Human Soul* and the question is whether innocence and experience can in any sense co-exist as the quotation from *The Marriage* suggests they might, or whether there is an inevitable progression from innocence, which must always be destroyed, to experience. When originally placed in *Innocence, The Voice of the Ancient Bard* must have sounded a note of warning with its reference to *clouds of reason*, and yet its tone is optimistic. It appears to make better sense at the end of *Experience* where the *opening morn* offers hope in reply to the despair of the Earth *Chained in night* in *Earth's Answer*. Nevertheless the optimism is not glib, for it recognizes the *Tangled roots* of the world of experience and acknowledges *How many have fallen there. To*

Tirzah also speaks of the constraints of material existence, but seems to offer hope in that Jesus, the *Divine Human* of whom Swedenborg speaks, sets him free and so man is *Raised a Spiritual Body*. It is open to argument as to whether this can be seen as a *progression* to a deeper level of feeling in which innocence and experience, both *necessary to human existence*, are resolved together.

Perhaps it would be more in the spirit of Blake to finish not with reasoning, but with two images, one visual and one verbal. The title page of the combined *Songs* shows Adam and Eve wearing the clothes made from fig leaves that denote their lost innocence, and cowering away from the flames that are driving them from the Garden of Eden. Flying away above the flames is a bird which perhaps represents innocence. Are we to put the stress on the separation of innocence from Adam and Eve for ever, or to see that innocence finally escapes from the flames of experience?

Finally there is the image of the Tiger. Here is all the energy which Blake so admired and which is surely a part of experience, and here also is a beauty which can be found in innocence as well. Perhaps the *Contrary States* do combine and the answer should be 'Yes' to Blake's question:

Did he who made the Lamb make thee?

Nevertheless there can be no final answer, for the poetry is too complex to be susceptible to any easy explanation. That is why each of the several approaches that has been touched on here needs to be applied. The initial impact of rhythm and imagery should never be overlooked and nor should the wider associations of the imagery and each poem's relationship to the rest of the *Songs*. At the same time you need to bear in mind the revolutionary times in which Blake lived, as well as his own far from orthodox thoughts and reactions. In your own personal response you must be prepared to hold in creative tension the various possible readings which, taken together, make Blake's poetry so richly satisfying.

127

Chronology

This chronology is only intended to give a few of the more important events in Blake's life. It gives less detail of events after the production of the combined *Songs of Innocence and of Experience* and in particular it mentions little of the enormous number of prints, drawings and paintings which were a major part of Blake's artistic output and the means by which he earned a living.

Events in Blake's life

1757	Born 28 November to James Blake, a hosier, and Catherine.
1767	Youngest and favourite brother, Robert, born. Starts to attend Pars' drawing school
1772	Apprenticed to the engraver, Henry Basire.
1774-6	Probably helped Basire with plates for Bryant's *Ancient Mythology*.
1777	Completes poems later printed in *Poetical Sketches*.
1779	Studies at Royal Academy where he drew from antique and from living models, but disliked the latter.

Historical events

1762	Rousseau: *Du Contrat Social* and *Émile*.
1775	American War of Independence begins.
1776	Thomas Paine: *Common Sense*.
1779	Cowper and Newton: *Olney Hymns*.

Events in Blake's life

1794	*Songs of Innocence and of Experience* produced as single volume. *Europe* and *Book of Urizen* engraved.
1795	*Song of Los, Book of Ahania,* and *Book of Los* engraved.
1803	Turns soldier out of his garden and is accused by him of sedition.
1804	Trial and acquittal. Probably finishes writing *Milton*.
1810	Finishes engraving first version of *Milton*. Over next two years finishes writing *The Four Zoas*.
1815	Blake reduced to engraving for Wedgwood's china catalogues.
1820	First copy of *Jerusalem* printed.
1822	*The Ghost of Abel* printed (the last illuminated book).
1827	Dies 12 August.
1831	Catherine Blake dies 18 October.

Historical events

1803	War with France resumed after peace of previous year.
1804	Napoleon becomes Emperor. First Corn Laws.
1810	British trade in slaves abolished.
1815	End of Napoleonic Wars with Battle of Waterloo.
1820	Shelley: *Prometheus Unbound, Oedipus Tyrannus.* Keats: *Lamia and Other Poems.*
1822	Byron: *Vision of Judgement.*
1827	Tennyson's first poems published.
1833	Parliament abolishes slavery throughout the Empire.
1875	Chimney sweeping by children abolished.

Historical events

1787	Association for Abolition of Slavery founded.
1789	French Revolution starts.
1790	Edmund Burke: *Reflections on the Revolution in France*.
1791	Unsuccessful attempt to pass bill to abolish slavery. Thomas Paine: *Rights of Man*.
1792	Commons pass motion calling for end of the slave trade.
1793	Louis XIV executed. France declares war on Britain.
1794	Fall of Robespierre. Paley: *Evidences of Christianity*.
1798	Coleridge: 'France. An Ode' and, with Wordsworth: *Lyrical Ballads*.

Events in Blake's life

1780	Present at burning of Newgate Prison during Gordon No-Popery Riots.
1782	Marries Catherine Boucher (illiterate).
1783	*Poetical Sketches* printed, but not published.
1784	Father dies. Starts print shop with James Parker as partner. Writes *An Island in the Moon* (prose satire interspersed with poems).
1785	Ends partnership in print shop.
1787	Robert Blake (brother) dies.
1788–9	Writes *Tiriel*.
1789	Engraves *Thel* and *Songs of Innocence*. Present at first London meeting of Swedenborgian New Church.
1790	Begins *Marriage of Heaven and Hell* at about this time.
1791	Proofs printed of first book of *French Revolution* (never completed or published).
1792	Blake's mother dies.
1793	*Visions of the Daughters of Albion* and *America* engraved.

Further Reading and Musical Settings

Editions

There is a paperback colour reproduction of the *Songs* which enables you to appreciate the poems as Blake originally intended his readers to: Geoffrey Keynes (ed.), *Blake, Songs of Innocence and of Experience* (Oxford University Press) 1970.

If you wish to read more widely in Blake then a clear edition with brief notes arranging the material thematically is: Michael Mason (ed.), *William Blake* (Oxford University Press) 1988.

Background

Mona Wilson, *The Life of William Blake* (Oxford University Press) 1971.

A good general introduction to the period is: J.R. Watson, *English Poetry of the Romantic Period 1789-1830* (Longman) 1985.

For a book specifically about Blake's own relation to a period of revolution see: J. Bronowski, *William Blake and the Age of Revolution* (Routledge and Kegan Paul) 1972.

A book which relates the *Songs* to Blake's own immediate surroundings and life is: Stanley Gardner, *Blake's* Innocence and Experience *Retraced* (St Martin) 1986.

Criticism

A general introduction to Blake's poetry for the new reader, with some comment on individual poems in the *Songs*, is Martin K. Nurmi, *William Blake* (Hutchinson) 1975.

There are some helpful general surveys of the *Songs* in the following collection of essays which between them contain quite detailed discussions of most of the more interesting and challenging of the poems: Margaret Bottrall (ed.), *William Blake, Songs of Innocence and Experience, A Casebook* (Macmillan) 1970.

A more difficult book, but particularly rewarding on *London* is: Edward Larrissy, *William Blake* (Oxford University Press) 1985.

Musical Settings

Blake is thought to have made up tunes for some of the *Songs*. If you are interested to hear how other composers have set the words to music then there are a number of interesting recordings:

Vaughan Williams's *Ten Blake Songs for Voice and Oboe* is particularly good in capturing the spirit of *Innocence* (EMI ED7691701, record: ED7691704, cassette);

Benjamin Britten's *Songs and Proverbs of William Blake* includes some powerful settings from *Experience* (Polygram 4173101, record; 4173104, cassette);

Benjamin Britten's setting of *The Sick Rose* in *Serenade* (the section called *Elegy*) is very evocative (a re-issue of a fine, early recording by the composer and Peter Pears and Barry Tuckwell: Decca 417 183-4, record and cassette; or a later recording with the same artists on CD, Decca 417 1532, or on record or cassette, 417 311-4);

John Tavener's hauntingly repetitive setting of *The Lamb* is on *More Christmas Music by Candlelight* by Ex Cathedra (Alpha APS 371 record only).

Tasks

1 Re-read *The Little Black Boy*, *Holy Thursday* and *The Chimney-Sweeper* in *Innocence*. Is it right to see in these poems something more than a portrayal of innocence? You may find it helpful to consider amongst other things the following:
   - historical facts about slaves, charity children and sweeps (see notes pp. 57, 60 and 62 and Approaches pp. 110-11 and 117-19);
   - alternative interpretations of the imagery;
   - irony;
   - voice – who are the characters who 'speak' the poems?

2 Blake claims that his *Songs* show the *Two Contrary States of the Human Soul*. Choose two or three pairs of 'contrary' poems and examine how they relate to each other. To what extent are the later poems a contradiction of the earlier ones and to what extent are they simply a development of them?

3 Examine Blake's use of imagery. You may find it useful to consider the following points:
   - the lack of detailed and particularized description in such poems as *Laughing Song* and *The Echoing Green*;
   - Blake's concept of vision (see p. 98);
   - his use of contemporary references;
   - his use of images from religion and myth;
   - his development of images through a series of poems.

4 'Blake's voice is the voice of freedom.' Do you agree with this claim? Support your answer by reference to both *Innocence* and *Experience*. Areas of freedom you might consider include:
   - moral;
   - financial;
   - religious;
   - political;

- sexual;
- between child and adult.

5   Blake varied the order of his poems as he prepared each individual copy. Arrange ten or twelve of the poems in an order that seems to you to be meaningful and explain how your order enables the poems to throw light on each other. You may mix poems from *Innocence* and *Experience* or select them from one only (you should note that some of the poems originally in *Innocence* were subsequently transferred to *Experience*).

6   Use some of the following comparisons between poems to help you decide what are the essential features of Blake's work. You should look for both similarities and differences in such matters as:
- themes;
- vocabulary and tone;
- imagery;
- rhythm.

a) Compare *Infant Joy, Infant Sorrow*, the extract given below from Joanna Baillie's *A Mother to her Waking Infant* and Richard Graves's *Maternal Despotism*. (You may also wish to refer to the two *Nurse's Songs*.) Which of the poems captures best the feelings of a mother? – and of a baby? Does outward realism necessarily mean that a poem is conveying a greater truth?

from *A Mother to her Waking Infant*

When sudden wakes the bitter shriek,
And redder swells thy little cheek;
When rattled keys thy woes beguile,
And through the wet eye gleams the smile,
Still for thy weakly self is spent
Thy little silly plaint.

But when thy friends are in distress,
Thou'lt laugh and chuckle ne'er the less;

Nor e'en with sympathy be smitten,
Though all are sad but thee and kitten;
Yet little varlet that thou art,
Thou twitchest at the heart.

(written 1790)

The next poem makes reference both to Paine's *Rights of Man* (see p. 114) and to Mary Wollstonecraft's *Rights of Woman* (a pioneering assertion of women's rights). The poem was written at a time when wrapping children in swaddling bands was becoming unfashionable in progressive circles.

Maternal Despotism; or, The Rights of Infants

Unhand me nurse! thou saucy quean!
What does this female tyrant mean?
Thus, head and foot, in swathes to bind,
'Spite of the 'Rights of human kind';
And lay me stretched upon my back
(Like a poor culprit on the rack);
An infant, like thyself born free,
And independent, slut! on thee.
Have I not right to kick and sprawl,
To laugh or cry, to squeak or squall!
Has ever, by my act or deed,
Thy right to rule me been decreed?
How dar'st thou, despot! then control
Th' exertions of a free-born soul?
Though now an infant, when I can,
I'll rise and seize 'The Rights of Man';
Nor make my haughty nurse alone,
But monarchs tremble, on their throne;
And boys and kings henceforth you'll see
Enjoy complete Equality.

(written 1792?)

b) Compare two or three of Blake's poems with one of the twentieth-century poems that follow on pages 136 and 137. Choose poems which have some similarity of theme or imagery.

Dreampoem

in a corner of my bedroom
    grew a tree
    a happytree
    my own tree
its leaves were soft
    like flesh
and its birds sang poems for me
then
    without warning
two men
    with understanding smiles
and axes
    made out of forged excuses
came and chopped it down
either   yesterday
    or the day before
i think it was the day before

Roger McGough

The Life of the Poet

Lock the door, Schoolmaster,
Keep the children in.
The river in spate at the schoolyard gate
Roars like original sin.

Watch your thermometer, Sister,
The patient refuses to die.
The dizzy germ and the raving sperm
Can't keep his powder dry.

Strike the drum, Bandmaster,
Under the rig of the moon.
The girls come whirling, their veils unfurling,
But what has become of the tune?

Answer the door, Squire,
Your manners are on the table.
There's a job to be done with a humane gun
If the horse is still in the stable.

Draw your revolver, Banker,
Shoot him down like a dole.
You may gird his loins with nickel coins
But where's his immortal soul?

Open the book, Parson,
See whom you will save.
They say you're as kind as an open mind
Or an open grave.

Fall out, fall out, Gabriel,
You might as well hit the hay.
Your visitor wears the spinning airs
And won't be round today.

Charles Causley

c) Compare *London* with this earlier draft by Blake (deletions
are in brackets and marked *del*). What light is thrown on the
final version by seeing which words and phrases of the earlier
version Blake rejected and which ones he kept?

I wander thro' each dirty street,
Near where the dirty Thames does flow,
And (see *del*) mark in every face I meet
Marks of weakness, marks of woe.

In every cry of every man
In (every voice of every child *del*)
   every infant's cry of fear
In every voice, in every ban
The (german[1] *del*) mind forg'd (links I hear *del*)
               manacles I hear.

---

1 The meaning of *german* is *closely related*.

(But most *del*) How the chimney sweeper's cry
(Blackens o'er the churches' walls, *del*)
Every black'ning church appalls,
And the hapless soldier's sigh
Runs in blood down palace walls.

(But most the midnight harlot's curse
From every dismal street I hear,
Weaves around the marriage hearse
And blasts the new born infant's tear. *del*)

But most (from every *del*) thro' wintry streets I hear
How the midnight harlot's curse
Blasts the new born infant's tear,
And (hangs *del*) smites with plagues the marriage hearse.

But most the shrieks of youth I hear
But most thro' midnight & . . .
How the youthful . . .

7   Write an additional verse for one of the *Songs*. You should try
     to match rhythm, rhyme, imagery and, of course, subject
     matter. Now write a parody of part of the same poem
     (*Maternal Despotism* above provides an illustration of how
     ideas such as Blake's may be parodied, but try to parody
     imagery and verse form as well). What have you learnt about
     the *Songs* as a result of this exercise?

8   Prepare a sequence of some of the *Songs* for performance to
     the rest of your group. Give thought to stress, pace and tone.
     Do you need different voices for different poems or within
     certain poems? Try to find musical settings of some of the
     Songs (for suggestions see p. 132). How far do these settings
     change or enhance your own readings of the poems?

9   Look at Blake's illustrations to the *Songs*. To what extent are
       they merely illustrations of the text and to what extent do
       they convey an additional meaning? You may like to look at
       other prints and paintings of the period which illustrate
       Blake's times (e.g. prints of events such as the fall of the
       Bastille or the execution of Louis XIV, satirical and political
       prints by the successors of Hogarth, whose work is also well
       worth examining, and the etchings and paintings of Goya).

10   Experiment with presenting Blake's ideas in diagram form.
       For example, you might place the word 'child' at the centre
       of a circle and write on the circumference those who influ-
       ence the child, linking them to the centre by writing on the
       radii the various pressures that are brought to bear on the
       child. Alternatively, you might create a web illustrating the
       associations of a key image such as the green, or the rose and
       thorns. (Beware of letting an attractive pattern seduce you
       into schematizing your material too rigidly.)

11   Imagine the year below you are just about to start studying
       Blake and prepare a talk explaining the difficulties you first
       found in reading the *Songs* and the strategies you used to
       overcome them. Did you, for example, find it helpful
       concentrate on:
       • key images,
       • comparing 'contrary' poems;
       • linking ideas and images from one poem to another;
       • 'performing' the poems;
       • relating the poems to their background?

Infant Joy

These plates are a selection of Blake's own engravings for the *Songs*.
Note the annunciation-like scene within the shelter of the opened, but
protective, flower.

Nurse's Song (Experience)

The children look submissive and apathetic, but the luxuriant vines perhaps suggest the untasted delights of the outside world.

The Sick Rose

The SICK ROSE

O Rose thou art sick.
The invisible worm.
That flies in the night
In the howling storm:

Has found out thy bed
Of crimson joy:
And his dark secret love
Does thy life destroy.

Note the figure (perhaps denoting life or joy?) leaving the rose as the worm penetrates it, and also the caterpillar (top left) and the 2 despairing figures (male and female?) caught on the sharp thorns.

The Fly

Both the mother and dead-looking branch bend oppressively over the boy, while the girl is left to play without a partner.

The Tiger

How successful is Blake in portraying the Tiger's *fearful symmetry*?

To Tirzah

The old man's robe carries a quotation from St Paul's teaching about the resurrection of the body: *It is sown a natural body: it is raised a spiritual body,* just as the seed is buried (i.e. sown) and dies to make possible a new and different life. Presumably the jug contains the water of life.

Index of Titles and First Lines